4th Edition

Cover Image by Tom Reichner/Shutterstock.com
Back Cover Image by Bryan Campell/Shutterstock.com

ISBN 1451574215
EAN-13 9781451574210

For my family

This book is dedicated to my family, my parents who have always believed in me and my children Dalton and Abigail who constantly give me reason to better myself.

Special thanks to

My neighbor Marty for the support, and all the authors, hunters, and friends who keep us all dreaming about elk season throughout the year.

Table of Contents

Preface

Introduction

If you're new to elk hunting, welcome. If you've got a few years under your belt, you know how utterly addictive this sport can be, and utterly frustrating as well. The path I followed was the same as most hunters I've spoken with, I started with very little knowledge and nobody to show me the ropes. I went on hunting trips with friends and family hoping to glean a few morsels of elk hunting know-how and ended up feeling that even some of the more senior hunters knew less than I did and were just guessing like the rest of us. After recently attending an elk hunting seminar put on by a local organization which consisted of about 75% novice elk hunters, I felt for the attendees who came without any idea of where to find an elk, and left with pretty much the same. One participant even stood up and asked the very pointed question, "How exactly do I go about finding a good place to hunt elk" which was met with the age old generic response of "find food, cover, and water on a map". I don't know about the rest of you, but I haven't been able to find the perfect map that shows me exactly where the elk's food is and where they bed during the day. To make matters worse, it seems that every square inch on the maps I've studied have some sort of blue line representing a stream or river running through them. So how exactly does one go about increasing their odds for harvesting an elk?

1

Jumpstart Elk Hunting

Although I don't remember where I heard it, I've always remembered a phrase about elk, "the elk are where the elk are". Anyone who has spent years in the field chasing these animals understands exactly what that means. It means they are where they want to be, not where you want them to be. Elk are mysterious creatures; however they're not altogether unpredictable. No book can guarantee you 100% success, and even if you paid $5000 for a hunt on a private ranch, there's still a chance you'll come up empty handed. The best we as hunters can do is to acquire all the knowledge that we can, apply it to the task at hand, and hope that our efforts pay off. Getting the knowledge though is often the hard part. I read a book at one point that said a serious hunter should spend no less than 100 days out of the year scouting and planning their hunt. I don't know about you, but I have a job, a mortgage, and mouths to feed that aren't going to be quite as understanding about my yearly elk hunting obsession. Most of us get a weekend, perhaps even a week out of the year to go out and chase these creatures, and we need all the help we can get. This book is meant for the rest of us. The folks who work for a living, and get a precious few days out of the year to go up with our friends and family and hunt elk.

This book is not all inclusive about every facet of elk hunting, in fact, most books that I've seen are filled with page after page of generic information that repeats from book to book. A few nuggets of helpful information exist, but most of us forget these things from year to year and we then fall back into our old habits of hunting areas that we've hunted in the past without success, or planning to hunt a spot we heard about from a buddy.

Using this Book

For those hunters who don't have time to re-read all their elk hunting books each year, this book is written to give the most helpful and important points you'll need to increase your odds of success each year. You can skim the jumpstart sections at the end of each chapter prior to your season for a refresher to remind you of the key information you need to have in your head. You may also want to take this book with you when you go, just in case you need to work yourself through the steps when things aren't going the way you want them to.

The goals of this book are simple but important. I believe whole-heartedly that the longer you're in the field, the better your chances of killing an elk. It's important to understand that each section is written with one of two goals in mind: either to ensure that you maximize the number of hours spent hunting or to help you hunt higher probability areas. If you're tempted to skip the initial sections on preparation and gear, don't. Most of the hunters I've seen return to camp early have reasons revolving around being tired, hungry, or uncomfortable (or all of the above). The difference between spending twelve hours in the field versus eight or hiking in four miles versus two equate to 50% greater opportunity for success when it comes to elk hunting and these sections were written specifically to help ensure that you minimize negative factors.

Regarding hunting areas, obviously the more elk within your chosen hunting grounds the better your chances of running into one. Elk can be anywhere at any given time; however if you can hunt an area that holds ten elk per square mile versus five you've just doubled your chances filling your cooler with meat.

In short, this book is intended to cut through the "bull" and jump start your success in elk hunting.

1

Chapter 1: Preparation

Preparation for elk hunting should start months in advance of your actual hunting date. It will take dedication on your part to work through the steps required to increase your chances for success. Many of the exercises we'll walk through take time, and performing activities like sighting in your rifle and talking to wildlife specialists are best done well in advance, before the masses of other hunters begin performing their last minute preparations. The amount of preparation you do is up to you; just know that like anything else, the more you invest, the more you get out.

Setting Expectations

I'm a meat hunter. Not being particularly concerned with calling in a 350 class bull (although I have no objection to that); I'll shoot the first legal elk that crosses my path. I know this about myself and haven't once regretted making a shot on a cow or smaller bull.

Even in years where I shot a cow on opening morning, then had a six point cross my path the next day when calling for my buddy, I haven't regretted fulfilling my goal of having meat in the cooler at the end of a hard day's hunting. It's important to set expectations for your hunt based on several factors such as what you want out of your trip, how long you're staying, what the area holds, etc. If you decide early that the reason you're going is to fill the freezer, then the decision is simple. If you really need something to fill that big empty spot over the mantle, well, that will change some factors of your approach that we'll discuss later in data scouting.

The most important expectation to set though is truly around your success. Nobody I know is successful 100% of the time, and even those addictive hunting videos we watch that show seasoned elk hunting veterans surrounded by bugling bulls, aren't typically filmed in a weekend. Many of the scenarios we're "sold" on television and video are on private ranches, or if they are hunting public land, listen closely, I've heard them exclaim many times that they're on day five or six of their hunt, and I guarantee you these guys are hunting hard.

It's important to set out with every expectation of being successful. Make sure you're prepared to spend the day in the field, execute a good shot, and get your animal back to camp and eventually home. If you're not successful, don't beat yourself up about it. If you had the opportunity to bask in some beautiful scenery, strengthened your body with some valuable exercise, and spent some quality time with friends or family, you were already successful, the rest is gravy.

Types of Trips

Most hunters I know are lucky to get a weekend to go hunting; some may even save up their vacation for a week-long trip during archery season. Here in Colorado, archery runs for about a month, and most of the rifle seasons are much shorter, around 4 -5 days in duration. The type of trip you intend to take will dictate some of the factors around how you prepare for it. The following section will cover preparation for three types of trips: weekend, week, and extended (being anything over a week). I've come to understand beyond doubt that preparation is directly linked to success. It's not just about avoiding finding yourself without a critical piece of gear, preparation extends far beyond equipment. Preparation and planning will help ensure that you're rested, prepared, and in the best mental state possible during your hunt. If you're tired and don't want to get up early, you're likely going to miss an opportunity. If you find yourself in the field with your stomach complaining about its empty state, you're likely to head back to camp earlier and miss a bull that another hunter jumped from his bed. Success is where preparation meets opportunity and when it comes to elk hunting, you'll want every possible edge you can get.

Weekend

Weekend trips require much less in the way of preparation and I strongly encourage folks to take it easy on themselves when preparing for items such as shelter, clothing, and food. If there's a hotel in a nearby town, you may want to consider shelling out a few bucks for some comfortable and convenient lodging during your short stay. It's much easier than setting up and breaking down even the smallest of camps. If you don't have the advantage of nearby lodging (or don't want it), the following information may prove useful:

Setting up a base camp

Having spent many uncomfortable nights fighting for room in a small mummy style sleeping bag, I'm convinced that one of the most important purchases you can make is an excellent quality sleeping bag rated between 0 and -30 degrees with inside lining made of flannel. I can do without many things, and can tolerate a lot, but being cold is just not for me. Even a night in a small, nylon style tent that holds little heat will provide a warm and cushioned environment under all but the most extreme conditions with such a bag. I have a medium sized nylon tent that I can put up in about 5 minutes, and a larger wall tent that can house a wood burning stove. The latter is just too much to set up and tear down for a weekend so the medium tent does the job just fine with a little propane heater running next to my bag when it snows. A helpful tip to ensure a comfortable night's sleep is to get an inexpensive pillow and keep it rolled up inside your bag. Having a soft resting place to keep your head slightly elevated makes a world of difference.

Cooking

This is another arena where it seems no matter how extensive your cooking preparations and plans are, morning seems to arrive too early and chances are you'll be exhausted when you arrive back at camp. Take this into account when you're planning for the preparation of your food and you'll see that it's possible to have a satisfying meal without too much effort. Breakfast bars, bagels, or cinnamon rolls may not be as warming as a hot bowl of oatmeal, but they're so much easier and you'll want to squeeze every drop of sleep that you can out of your nights. As a self-proclaimed coffee addict and snob, it's hard for me to go without a good cup of coffee in the morning. I actually begin to get a headache at high altitudes without caffeine. The small single serving packets of instant coffee are very convenient and all you have to do then is heat up some water. In fact, it seems that Starbucks has even taken pity on the hunting population and begun producing single serve packets of excellent instant coffee.

When you get back to camp, you should be too tired to cook. This is a good sign! It means you spent your time doing what you were supposed to be doing which is hiking and hunting; however not much can compare to a hot meal at the end of a long day. Two items are now a staple for my trips, either freeze dried dinners where you just add hot water, or the "meal in a bag" skillet dinners that they sell in the grocery stores. Make sure they're actually single skillet meals as many of them are for the oven or crock pot, but if you look you'll find quite a few choices. Having everything in one bag, heating it quickly, and then washing a single pan afterwards makes an easy and satisfying finish to a day of hunting. There are quite a few choices from pasta dishes, to beef stew, to chicken cacciatore. Choose what you like, just try to make it easy on yourself. I've also had good luck cooking my meals ahead of time and freezing them. Some don't work out as well as one might think (my spaghetti disaster comes to mind), but many items can be either reheated in a pan or boiled in the bag to provide a hot meal quickly.

Staying Clean

Elk have an excellent sense of smell, there's no denying that. The most powerful comment I ever heard about an elk's sense of smell and humans was that "we smell as strong to them as a skunk does to us". Without going too far into the "hunt the wind" speech, one way or another you're going to give off some scent, the best you'll be able to do is to minimize it. The stronger we smell, the better the odds for the elk. The areas on the human body that create the most bacteria to give off sent are the armpits and the groin area. If you're doing a weekend trip and going minimal, at very least try to clean these areas daily with unscented soap and water. Another handy item is a package of unscented wipes to clean your high scent areas after hiking to your spot, during the day, and in the morning before you go out.

Week Trip/Extended Trip

Most all of the items mentioned above can be used on any length of trip, however if you're going to be out in the field for an extended period of time, it's best to be comfortable. Base camp at this point can become a little more elaborate and make your trip much more pleasant.

Base Camp

Depending on the weather, you may wish to bring a tent that's a little sturdier. No matter how great your heater is, heat won't hold in a nylon tent and you run the risk of setting fire to it. There are quite a few options available to the hunter including small outfitter tents which set up with very few poles and some rope. If you look around your army surplus stores and on craigslist.com, you're bound to find quite a few used surplus tents. I used to own a 5 man arctic tent model with a 4 inch stove pipe outlet. It was very easy to set up alone with a single pole and some stakes. With a surplus wood burning stove in there, it had actually been a little too toasty on a few unseasonably warm summer nights. I have since upgraded to a full outfitter tent as they're not as difficult to set up and tear down as you might imagine.

Full outfitter tents are very nice, but depending on your budget, may be out of reach. If you tend to hunt with multiple people, you and your hunting buddies may want to consider splitting the cost of a tent. Just remember, buy one size bigger than you think you're going to need. I purchased a 12x14 tent from Davis Tent in Colorado. I can't say enough good things about the quality of the tent and the helpfulness of the owners. There's no commission involved in anything I recommend, but I'll freely share when I find a quality product backed by good service. The tent can be set up in under 30 minutes by a single person and the comfort and quality are next to none. Another option is to check out sites such as craigslist.com on your computer a few months before hunting season. I've seen several people renting out their outfitter tents at a fraction of what purchasing one would cost.

Other nice additions include a small shower pump so you can fill a bucket or container with warm water and really wash down. I bought a Coleman one for about $20 or Zodi sells a fully contained shower unit that runs off propane bottles for about $125. Add a 5 gallon bucket and I can take a nice hot shower right at camp.

Lastly, consider buying a good cot to sleep on and a pad for under your sleeping bag. I'll never forget the first night I slept in comfort that equaled my bed at home. You won't believe the difference it will make at night and in the morning when it's time to get up. The only risk is that you'll be so comfortable; you won't want to get out of bed.

Cooking

Once again, regardless of how long you're there, if you're hunting all day, you're going to be tired when you get back. Spending excessive time and energy cooking a meal is likely the last thing you'll want to do. For a week or more, it's worth it to bring a propane cooking stove that hooks to a full propane bottle such as the kind on your BBQ. The little units with the portable propane bottles will work, but if you plan things right, you can use the propane for multiple conveniences such as cooking your food, heating water quickly, and heating your tent at night. Most sporting goods stores have effective single burner units for under $50, and if you're a bargain hunter, you can find some standing dual burner stoves for under a hundred.

Packing

Packing has become an art to me; it's the difference between a stressful and disorganized hunt and one where I'm well prepared and focused on the day ahead of me. There are a few tricks that will help you stay organized and ensure that you'll be well prepared to head out the next morning. Remember to pack in the opposite order of what you'll need and when you'll need it during your hunt. If you have extra layers of clothing that you intend to put on when you get to your spot, those are the last items to go in your pack as you'll be pulling them out first.

Clothing

As you get your clothes together for your hunt, here's a handy trick. Lay out a pair of pants, fold a shirt in half and lay it on the pants, then add a single pair of underwear and a single pair of socks to the bottom half. You can add more layers too if you know you'll need them first thing in the morning as well. Take your pile of clothes you've set out, and roll it up from the bottom to the top and slip a large rubber band over the bundle. Make one bundle for each day and when you get up in the morning you'll have everything you need and won't have to go searching for anything. I pack all my rolls into a plastic bin that I keep my raingear, gaiters, and extra socks in the bottom of. With one tote, I'm ready for rain or shine and can easily grab a roll of clothes the night before and have them sitting next to me in the tent the next morning.

Another point on clothing, if you're hiking up to a spot that's miles away and uphill, it doesn't matter how cold it is when you leave camp, you're going to sweat. I prefer to be slightly cold once dressed in these situations with extra layers in my pack for when I get to my spot. By the time I'm halfway up the mountain, I'm usually looking for somewhere to store my hat and gloves as I begin to heat up. Take this into consideration when you get ready to leave in the morning and consider keeping your warmer clothes in your pack.

Field dressing gear

I have everything I need to field dress and bone out my animal stored in a small shaving kit bag that I picked up at Wal-Mart for $5. I make sure it's full every trip and then throw it in the bottom of my pack. Notice I said the bottom. It's the last thing I'll need on a successful elk hunt and therefore it goes in the most inaccessible part of my pack. One of these small 8 inch by 6 inch bags will hold a folding knife, gloves, pillow cases, drop cloth, etc. with ease and keeps everything from rattling around in my pack.

Food

If you get too hungry, chances are you won't stay in the field. It will be one more reason you'll think about in favor of heading back to camp when you haven't seen anything for hours and your faith begins to wane. Elk are on their own schedule and although they will follow patterns, they can be less than perfectly predictable and have a tendency to change their behavior. Your elk may come through at 6:00AM and may come through at 2:00 in the afternoon, but one thing is for sure, if you're not there, you won't kill it. The more prepared you are to stay in the field the longer you'll be out and the better your chances for success.

When packing food, I do most of the work while I'm at home. I plan my day's meals, usually consisting of two sandwiches, a baggie of trail mix, some beef jerky, and perhaps some cheese and cracker packs. I also throw in a couple of chemical hand warmers (unopened of course) to ensure I don't forget them. Each day's "ration" goes into a single gallon sized Ziploc bag or plastic grocery bag and into the cooler. This is my "refillable" package. Each morning I get up, grab my roll of clothing and put it on, grab my pack, throw a bag of food in from the cooler, fill my hydration pack and I'm ready to go. No searching for my granola bars, no trying to figure out if my sandwiches are hiding under the soft drinks, it's simple and I can be prepared in no time which allows me more time to sleep. I don't worry at night if I'm forgetting something as I crawl into my sleeping bag; I hop in and doze off. Follow this methodology and you'll find yourself with more time, better rested, and more focused.

Physical Conditioning

The last topic we'll touch on is being in shape to go out elk hunting. I'm not going to outline a full exercise regime for you as I've seen in other books on elk hunting. I know nothing about you, your current level of fitness, or any special circumstances that may exist. Just know that elk hunting is tough and to know your limitations. It is true that the further you get away from the roads and the deeper you get into the woods, the more likely you are to bag an elk. If you're in exceptional shape, by all means push the envelope, if not, then try to plan for that reality when you're look-ing for spots to elk hunt. You may find and absolute honey hole that you just know will hold elk, but its 5 miles downhill in steep terrain which means anything you bag, you'll be hauling out uphill. That might not be the best place for you to try and get into.

Jumpstart Elk Hunting

Your legs are the most important set of muscles in your body when it comes to elk hunting, you'll put more miles on them, add loads they're not used to carrying, and push them beyond what they're normally used to. Keep that fact in mind when you prepare yourself physically for your hunts. Lastly on this topic, if you're coming to hunt elk at elevations your body isn't used to, begin to prepare several days in advance by drinking a lot of water, and I do mean a lot. Drink your 8-10 glasses a day minimum plus extra, and be sure to drink plenty of water once you arrive. This doesn't come so much from my elk hunting experience as it does from working in a training facility many years back. People from all over the US would fly into Colorado and end up missing the first day of training from altitude sickness.

Obviously year round exercise will keep your body healthy and the daily climb up mountainous terrain won't seem so taxing. If you don't have the time or the discipline to exercise year round, at very least start 60 days prior to your trip. If you can manage to run a mile three times a week, building up if you can't run the full mile at first, then you'll be physically ready for most average elk hunts.

Jumpstart Chapter 1

- Set expectations for your hunt based on time, your expectations, bull/cow ratios and herd statistics for your area
- Set up a camp that's comfortable and convenient for your length of stay
- Prepare as much food as possible ahead of time or buy bagged "one skillet" meals for easy, hot dinners
- Make sure you're prepared to spend the entire day in the field, more elk are harvested after 4PM than in the morning and afternoon hours
- Try to keep clean each day, especially the armpits and groin areas
- Pack your daily rations and more food than you think you'll need for each day ahead of time. Morning should be "grab and go"
- Pack your gear in the opposite order of when you'll need it
- Try to leave camp in the morning dressed to be slightly cold, you'll heat up quickly once moving
- Bring enough food to ensure you won't be hungry during the day, many snacks are better than large meals
- If you're coming from a lower altitude area, drink as much water as possible right before and during your trip
- At very least, begin your workout regime 60 days prior to your trip to ensure you're physically prepared

Chapter 2: Gear

I've often thought that if by some chance we're judged in the next life by the amount of hunting gear that we accumulate, I'm going to heaven for sure. Yes I'll admit, I'm a sucker for cool hunting gadgets and items that I convince myself will make me more successful or more comfortable. Some of them work, some of them don't (at least not for me) and I'll share that with you later. In the meantime, I'd like to share with you my golden rule of gear, "Bring it." I can't tell you how many times in the past I've thought as I looked at an extra set of cold weather boots or some rain gear and thought, "Nah, I won't need that." You never know for certain what you will and won't need in the field. Getting up in the morning to find rain pouring down during you summer archery hunt is no time to remember that it's sitting at home. If you bought it, and there's even a remote chance that you'll need it, bring it.

Organizing your gear at Home

It's easier than you think to bring all the things you'll need if you organize your gear accordingly. Not only will you have what you need when you need it, but if you're married, your wife will appreciate the lack of hunting clutter spread across the garage and basement. I classify and organize my gear into several categories:

Standard: This is the gear you'll need on any hunt regardless of season. Keeping all of these items together will allow you to grab a single plastic tote and know that you have most of the items you'll need. Items that fall into this category include things like your GPS, walkie-talkie, field dressing gear, survival items, extra batteries, calls, flashlight, etc. Later in the section on how to pack, we'll look at how to keep these items together so they're easily transferable between packs (you do own more than one right?), and near impossible to forget. As you build your elk hunting checklist, you'll find more items that fall into this category, that's great, you can keep adding as you please until you have one tote with the common items you'll need no matter if you're hunting archery, rifle, or muzzleloader.

Archery: As the name implies, this is where all your archery gear goes. Items such as broadheads, extra release, bow tools (hex wrench, bow scale, etc.) bow hanger, collapsible decoy, and other archery specific items go. Be sure you're ready to address any issues that may arise with your bow from this box. I've had it happen to me many times where my bow was shooting perfect when I left, only to be off when I got to camp. Having your tools with you to re-nock your string or adjust your rest can be a lifesaver.

Rifle: I've acquired quite a lot of rifle gear over the years, and I hunt many different species including elk, deer, antelope, and varmint to name a few, so it's up to you whether or not you want to break some of these down into smaller totes. Personally, I have one tote that has everything I need for rifle as it all fits nicely in the single tote. My rifle box contains items such as shooting sticks, sling(s) clips, gun cleaning kit, neoprene gun covers, and the like. We'll go deeper into all the necessary gear in "How to pack", but the idea is to have one tote that you can easily load into the truck and go without worry of forgetting something.

Later in this chapter, I'll get you started with my elk hunting checklist. I keep this on my computer and take it out every year prior to leaving on any trip. I run off a copy and begin crossing out items as I put them in my pile of gear to bring for the trip, it truly puts my mind at ease not to have to remember everything and start from scratch each season. I also update the list immediately with any items I wished I had while out in the field but were not included. Do it while it's fresh in your head and pretty soon you'll have a very complete list to ensure a great hunt.

Gearing up for your trip:

I had to laugh many years ago when I took a trip up to Cabela's, an outdoor sporting goods store that most hunters are familiar with. I wore a forest-green button down shirt without realizing that it was the exact color all the Cabela's employees wear. Twice I was approached while browsing hunting items asking for help in choosing gear. After explaining that I didn't work there, I offered my opinions which were very welcomed by these novice hunters. The point being is that when you start out, there are a million choices on gear and a million opinions to go with them. All I can do is offer my own based on my experience, you may find my preferences don't work for you, that's OK, but I've spoken to enough beginner elk hunters to know that most of them are lost and looking for some place to start, so here goes.

Pack(s)

I have multiple packs; each has a specific purpose and function to it that I've found invaluable in the field. I'm not a fan of the cheaper pack models; they'll get the job done, but lack specific features that will make a big difference. I have a very small pack for scouting (most of which I do in the summer), and a pack for archery and rifle. I'll discuss my specific preferences and why later in the "Gear Opinions" section, however just note that in most cases a good pack will make a big difference in your comfort and overall experience.

Archery

If you're going to hunt archery, you'll need a few items that are pretty obvious, and some that aren't so obvious but will make your hunt much more comfortable.

Bows: Bow technology changes about every 5 years or so, just something to be aware of. We've gone from round wheels, to hard cams, to split limbs, to the latest technology of parallel limbs. Personally, my favorite is the parallel limb design as it really does reduce hand shock and noise, but just remember that bows work by cutting and hemorrhaging. Any bow over 50lbs with a well-placed shot will do the trick, so if you're just starting out, consider looking on craigslist or eBay for a used bow.

Bows can be had for a decent price and you can gain valuable experience with most any bow that fits you well. If you have the money to burn though, PLEASE PLEASE PLEASE go down to a reputable sporting goods store or archery shop and at very least pull back on the bow, if they have an indoor range and you can shoot on it, all the better. I've pulled back on hundreds of bows and found very few that felt right. I felt like Goldilocks testing beds. "This one has too long of a valley, this one has too hard of a rollover, ahhh, this one is just right." If you don't know what I mean by these terms, I'll provide a quick and simple breakdown below, but you may wish to look in the references for a link to an excellent guide on choosing a bow.

Brace Height - Important - This is the distance from the riser (where you grip the bow) to the string. The longer the distance, the more forgiving the bow is to shooting form mistakes. The shorter it is, the faster your arrow will go, but any imperfection in form will affect your arrow. Beginners should get at least a 7" brace height.

Rollover - Moderately Important - When pulling back a compound bow, the wheels are offset to allow the bow to store more energy. Pulling back the bow will go from moderate at first, to much harder, then the let off kicks in and you're holding a fraction of what you were. There's no measurement that I'm aware of for rollover, it's just how it feels to you. One note though, you probably will have several times in the field where you're not pulling back the bow the same way you would at the range. You may be in a tree stand with limited movement range, or trying to pull back with minimal movement so as not to spook your target. Get one with a nice smooth rollover that you like, it will make those times easier.

Valley - Moderately Important - As stated above, the bow will go through multiple stages when drawing it back. The same happens when you let your arrow loose or let the bow down. There's a point called the valley where the bow goes from keeping the weight you're holding at a minimum, to an explosion of force propelling the arrow. Some bows seem to go from 0 to 60 in a millisecond (hard valley), some are much more gradual (soft valley). Its personal preference, but I'll highly recommend the hard valley for one important reason, it lets you know immediately if your string is creeping forward. An older bow of mine had a very soft valley and if I wasn't paying attention, would launch the arrow at less than full draw causing a low hit.

Speed - Moderately Important - Most folks get way too caught up in this. There's a tradeoff to everything in life, this is no exception. It's a general rule that more speed equals less forgiveness. This may not seem too important, however when you're in the field shooting from awkward positions, you'll want as much forgiveness as you can get.

There is an advantage to a faster bow in that you can be off on range estimation and perhaps still muster a hit, however if you're ranging objects where you expect the elk to come through, you'll already know the range.

My current bow was designed for hunting, not for target shooting. Most of the ads you'll see from bow manufacturers will try to sell you on how fast their model shoots. Although this may change in the future, I'm currently shooting a bow by Quest as they make hunting bows not target bows. The bow is designed for easy draw (important when you're drawing from awkward positions), high letoff and has a rock solid wall (important as I can hold this bow back effortlessly while elk are held up behind cover and I'm waiting for them to take that one more step). Even down to the design of the cable guards that can't fall off in the field as they're integral to the bow design. To me, all of this is much more important than having the fastest bow on the market or the one that looks the "coolest".

Arrows: Carbons are the way to go. Technology is changing a bit here too, you'll find newer arrows that are smaller in diameter than the typical arrows, some with proprietary inserts (where you screw the broad head in), and there's always a flavor of the month for vanes. Stick with the standard and you should be fine. I'd shy away from the non-standard or proprietary gimmicks as it will limit your choices on other matters such as a quiver (which I found out the hard way won't hold small diameter arrows) and broad heads.

Rests: I've tried and fiddled with more rests than I care to remember. All I can say is this, simple is better. I personally like drop away rests as there's very little adjustment required and they have the least affect on arrow flight once properly set up. Arrow clearance is one of the number one reasons arrows don't fly straight. Make sure yours are getting adequate clearance by spraying some gold bond foot powder liberally on the vanes of a single arrow, let it dry, and then shoot it. When you look at the vanes, any scrapes in the powder will be obvious allowing you to make adjustments. As a side note to this, don't try to tie these things in yourself, take it to the local bow shop or sporting goods store and let a pro do it. I tried and tried and every time they came undone.

Sights: Fiber optics are great. There are quite a few quality sights on the market, here are a few things I've found very useful in my experiences. Fiber optic sights come with a few different sizes of pins, the .029 are the way to go as they'll collect plenty of light and the vitals on an elk are large enough that you aren't going to cover too much of them with your pins. Single pin sights can break and then you're in trouble.

This happened to my hunting buddy last year when he was walking through the bushes to get to our spot. We did fix it by breaking off a piece and melting the end for a half a second with a lighter, but that turned me off of single pin sights right there. Lastly, for some reason, my bow never shoots in the field where it hit at the range. I bought a Tru-Glo 5 pin sight with tool-less adjustment, wow, what a sight! It holds excellent, is super bright, and I can make minor adjustments anywhere without a tool.

Broad heads: Fixed or expandable, that seems to be the question. Forever burned in my memory is a beautiful 6 point elk 50 yards across a meadow standing broadside. Also forever burned in my memory is the sight of my arrow making a perfect arc to the left and missing his tail by about an inch. I swore off fixed blades after that as I was convinced the blade caused my arrow to plane. It probably did, however it was more likely due to poor broad head alignment than it was the broad head itself.

I've taken elk with both fixed and expandable and both have worked well. If you don't get a clean pass through though, the expandable could close back up whereas the fixed will be acting as a food processor as the animal runs off. My personal favorite is a Magnus stinger 4 blade fixed. They shoot just like my field points, blood trails are excellent, and they're surgical sharp right out of the package. Take a permanent marker and write a small "p" on one for your practice blade so you know which one you used to check flight with as hitting a target tends to dull them.

Decoy: Archery is the only season I'd set foot in the woods with a decoy, but after getting one, I'll never hunt archery without one again. I use the Montana collapsible decoy and since beginning to use one, I've seen a marked difference in the elk's behavior when they come to my call.

Elk know exactly where you are when you call, and they expect to see another elk. Year after year when I'd call in elk, they'd come in and take an alert posture as they scanned for the source of the noise. This last year I missed a shot (right over her back) at an elk at 20 yards. She started to run and I immediately grabbed my call and let out a few lost cow mews as I had been doing. She turned around, walked right back by my decoy, put her head down and started to feed as I laced an arrow through both of her lungs. I'm convinced I wouldn't have had that opportunity without that decoy.

Just a tip on the decoys they offer, there are three of them. One called the COW ELK II (you'll recognize it as it is a side view) is the one I first bought and soon sent back in favor of the COW ELK original (alert) model. You must need a PhD in physics to fold that COW ELK II back up. The other two models fold up quite easily with a simple twist. Also, the stakes they come with are a bit heavy so if you heat up a tiny screwdriver with a lighter and burn a strategic hole through the top of the elk's head, you can put some heavy duty fishing line on it and presto, easy hanging from a tree.

Seat: Once we get into packing, you'll find I like to take the minimum amount of weight and gear that I have to in order to get the job done. This is one item I won't do without though. There are a few well-made tri-leg stools on the market that weigh very little and easily strap to the outside of your pack. I call elk in during archery season and this keeps me comfortable, and minimizes my movement should an elk appear unexpectedly. I recently purchased a swivel model seat that probably weighs about 3 pounds and is dead quiet.

Bow Hanger: The guy who thought this up is definitely getting into heaven. Keeping your bow at the ready while you sit for hours is a pain. This way you can hang your bow, your rangefinder, and your calls right in easy reach and minimize any movement when an elk sneaks in looking for you.

The one I prefer is the longer model that folds in half and allows you to hang other items such as a rangefinder and calls. If you're sitting against a tree, this model will keep your bow in perfect reaching distance. Also handy are the bow ground stakes that hold your bow from the bottom limb. The aluminum ones weigh very little and you can keep your bow right in front of you even if you have no tree to screw something into.

Rifle

The Perfect Elk Rifle: Is there such a thing? Try this, go to your favorite hunting forum and ask that question. You'll get about 20 replies, and half of those folks will be disagreeing with what the other guy said. I'll keep this one simple. Even smaller calibers such as a .270 or the popular 30-06 is suitable for elk. All different weights of ammos are available including 180-220 grain bullets that will have a lot of whump when they hit. These calibers will do the job just fine. If you're itching to buy a new elk rifle and are using this for an excuse, by all means do so.

For some reason, American hunters are convinced we need huge rounds to take down an elk. If you have some time, research the 6.5x55 Swedish Mauser round. It's used extensively in Europe and has an excellent track record for Scandinavian Moose. This round is .264 in diameter and usually weighs no more than 140 grains. Bullets kill by fragmentation with a well-placed shot, so it's not necessary to use a massive round to take an elk.

With that being said, not every shot is as well placed as we'd like it to be and sometimes having a little more energy is a comforting feeling. It also cannot be denied that a larger diameter bullet will create a larger wound channel and increases killing power. If I were to recommend a pure elk gun, I'd be looking at a .300 Winchester Magnum for the ability to shoot flat and keep a significant amount of energy at impact. Larger calibers such as the .338 are efficient for killing elk; however everyone I've spoken to has a terrible story about how punishing they are. Energy is where most of the discussions around an elk rifle will raise debate. Most calibers large enough to be considered by hunters for elk are flat shooting, high velocity rounds. Just as with arrows, the faster the bullet, the less drop at extreme yardages and also the greater the forgiveness for any range errors. We'll discuss later why in a shorter (100-300 yards) range shot, your bullet drop won't make much difference, however if you're shooting out past 300 yards, you should be using a rangefinder and range estimation won't enter into the equation.

Bullet energy is an important consideration in an elk rifle. The more energy at impact, the more damage the bullet is likely to do and shorter the distance until the elk falls. Most all well placed shots will drop and elk...eventually. The question is how far that elk goes before the damage finally brings the elk down and whether or not you'll be able to find it. A bullet with more energy at impact is going to do more damage and hopefully keep your harvest from going too far. Just make sure that the bullet you choose matches the round (more on that next).

The following table shows velocity and energy in foot pounds for some of the more common elk rifles including the 30-06 Springfield, the .300 Winchester Magnum, and the punishing .338 Winchester Magnum. All three of the calibers are being compared apples to apples with 180 grain bullets (sectional density excluded), although 200 grain bullets would be more common in a .338. Notice the higher energy and velocity of the .300 Winchester Magnum even compared to the larger .338. It's no wonder the .300 Winchester is one of the most popular elk calibers.

Weight	Type	Velociy					
		Muzzle	100 Y	200 Y	300 Y	400 Y	500 Y
180	30-06	2700	2500	2320	2140	1970	1810
180	300 Win Mag	2960	2760	2570	2380	2210	2040
180	.338	3120	2860	2380	2160	1950	1850

Weight	Type	Energy					
		Muzzle	100 Y	200 Y	300 Y	400 Y	500 Y
180	30-06	2915	2510	2150	1830	1550	1350
180	300 Win Mag	3500	3045	2635	2270	1950	1680
180	.338	3265	2900	2730	2265	1860	1520

Weight	Type	Trajectory				
		100 Y	200 Y	300 Y	400 Y	500 Y
180	30-06	+2.0	0	-8.6	-24.6	-49.6
180	300 Win Mag	+1.5	0	-6.8	-19.8	-39.8
180	.338	+1.4	0	-6.5	-19.1	-39.2

Many shooters are of the mindset that if a rifle has too much of a kick you won't shoot it as often and therefore you won't be as good of a shot. I agree with this to some extent, but much less with rifles than I do with pistols. In my experience, shooting is 90% form and the rest falls to other variables outside of the shooter's control. If you can shoot a .22 with extreme accuracy offhand, you'll do just as well with the .300 in theory, at least for the first few shots. The difference is our brain.

Our brain anticipates the punishing recoil of the rifle and causes us to destroy most of our good shooting form right as we pull the trigger. I used to worry about this quite a lot until I realized one thing. I can remember feeling the kick of my rifle every time EXCEPT for the times I was shooting at game. There are a few factors at work here. First of all, when you're at the range, chances are that you're sitting on a nice comfy bench and bracing yourself quite sturdily for the impact of the rifle. When you do this and pull the trigger, your body is going to absorb much more of the recoil in your shoulder than if your body could give a bit. Think of it like this, if you're standing against a wall and someone pushes you, you'll feel more of the push than you would if you were standing in the open and your body could move back a bit to decelerate the impact.

Most of the shots I've taken have been standing shots and I can't remember feeling any pain associated with making the shot. Some of that may be from the second factor which is your state of mind when you actually take the shot. When you're about to shoot, you'll be excited, trust me. Adrenaline will be pumping through your body and when you think back afterwards, you probably won't remember much about the actual shooting of your elk, you'll remember everything else.

I was terrified of my 30-06 when I first got it. I went to the range on a summer day with just a T-shirt on and tried to sight it in. After 10 shots, I physically couldn't move my finger to make the trigger pull again, my body had had enough. The next time I sighted it in was in the field before my first year elk hunting in

Colorado. We set up in the forest and I actually closed my eyes as I pulled the trigger. I remember distinctly thinking, "Huh, I didn't feel a thing." I shot several more times and nothing.

It took me a while to get over my fear, but now I don't think twice about it even when shooting my Remington .300 Ultra Mag, it's just not an issue. Lastly is the clothing you'll most likely be wearing in the field. Here in Colorado I'm well-padded during rifle season as many times there's snow on the ground. The layers of clothing act similar to a recoil pad by shielding your body from quite a bit of impact.

Please understand I'm not saying don't practice with the rifle you'll be hunting with. What I am saying though is that consistently practicing with it is expensive considering an average elk round costs about $2 each, and you'll get much more benefit from learning better shooting form by practicing with a .22 caliber rifle of similar weight.

While we're on the subject of shooting practice, I highly recommend that you take the time to learn shooting off-hand. Very few shots that I've taken have been from comfortable positions where I had an excellent rest to aid me in getting my crosshairs steady. If you can get your hands on a .22, go to a range that allows offhand shooting or to the forest where shooting is not prohibited, and spend some time learning to how to shoot like this. I can keep everything within the size of a quarter when my gun is in a sturdy rest and the range and all I have to do is pull the trigger, however it's completely different in the field. Another helpful practice aid is a pellet gun. I have a single barrel cocking .177

pellet gun that weighs 7.5lbs, the exact same as my rifle. I've practiced hundreds of time in my basement, shooting offhand into a phone book. It's excellent practice.

Rifle Action

Another consideration is the action of the gun. There are many types, however bolt action and semi auto are the most common. A semi-auto is a bit heavier and will absorb a bit more of the recoil, however I'm not a fan of semi autos in the least. They are not as accurate as a bolt action and I've never seen a bolt action jam. I've never actually seen a semi auto rifle jam either, but I've seen it many times with shotguns, sometimes at the most inopportune moments. I just tend to trust bolt actions more, and they're typically a much better value for your gun dollar.

Gun Finish

I have a fetish for beautiful wood stocks. They're so beautiful on that rack that once I do my research and settle in on a caliber I want, I have to fight myself to make sure I don't make the choice based on how pretty I think it is. The upside to getting a beautiful wooden stock on your firearm is that every time you take it out of the gun safe, you'll well up with the same pride and admiration as the day you bought it. The problem is out in the field. Hunting is tough and your precious beautiful firearm is bound to get scratched. Those scratches are heartbreaking. It has taken me a long time to finally break down and begin buying synthetic stocked rifles. They do hold up better than my wooden beauties, several of which have since been restocked due to abuse from the field.

If you're like me and you just can't resist the beautiful character of a fine piece of walnut, then consider investing in some no-mar type gun tape or even a neoprene skin for your baby. Some composite stocks make the gun lighter as well. Just understand the tradeoff, the lighter the gun the easier it is to carry in the field, but the more recoil you'll feel and vice-versa.

Rifle Scope

Just as with binoculars, the word on the street is to buy the best glass you can afford. Most books I've read recommend spending more on the scope than on the rifle. I've got all different kinds of scopes ranging from Japanese made top of the line scopes to discount glass that carries some buyer's remorse. I hunted for years with a higher end Tasco World Class scope and it performed flawlessly. I've never been able to justify the money for a Zeiss or Swarovski scope and having looked through them at sporting goods stores, I'm not sure I'm convinced that I'd spend several thousand dollars to be able to see a little better at dawn and dusk. Perhaps one day I'll regret that view if there's a massive trophy that I can barely make out in the last few minutes of shooting light, but as a meat hunter, I'm willing to take that chance.

I do think it's wise to invest in decent optics though, but I've never spent over $500 for any of my scopes and so far I haven't been let down. There are only a few things I'll suggest along the lines of buying a scope. First, I usually don't buy anything under 44mm objective lens diameter. For some reason, the 40 and 42mm objectives just create too small of a sight picture for me. I also like higher magnification capabilities, so a 4-12X or 4-16X scope is my preference. I always keep it down to 4X when I'm walking, but if I set up for a longer shot and have a good sturdy rest, the ability to go up higher for better shot placement is important to me. I don't care too much for scopes with an adjustable parallax, that's just one more thing to fidget with when a shot opportunity presents itself. Do your research on discussion boards and you'll likely find some great bargains out there.

I recently bought a Nitrex scope for my .300 Winchester Elk rifle. I've been pleased as punch with this scope and come to find out they were made by Weaver, a well-respected name in the world of optics.

Once you've bought your scope, make sure the rings you buy fit it correctly. I never quite understood this until I bought some extra high rings once and had an awkward "cheek weld" on my rifle. When you bring your gun up to shoot, you should have a sturdy "weld" from your cheek to the stock of your gun. If you have to raise your head up to see through a scope that's too high, accuracy will likely suffer. Find rings that put the scope as close to the barrel of the rifle as possible without risk of the two surfaces touching.

Triggers and trigger adjustment

Just about any gun you buy, inherit, or own is going to have a built in lawyer that came with it. Gun manufacturers these days are so concerned about a potential lawsuit that you'll most likely be pulling anywhere from 10 to 12 pounds of trigger pressure on an average big game rifle. It's near impossible to squeeze a round off with that much trigger resistance and not begin to move your point of aim, even on a sturdy rest. To give you an idea, most competition shooters shoot with triggers ranging from 1.5 to 3lbs triggers.

I've adjusted every trigger I own down to about 3lbs and many of my friends have asked me to do the same for them. Please note, if you don't feel comfortable executing this type of adjustment then please don't. Any type of trigger adjustment that involves anything other than finely polishing the sear and hammer or turning one or more adjustment screws typically involves trigger geometry and I just won't play with it. If you don't feel confident, take your gun to a qualified gunsmith and pay them to adjust your trigger. Depending on the rifle, it's most likely a small job and it will make a world of difference.

Now if you just can't keep your hands from tinkering with everything, many triggers are quite easy to adjust. The first thing I'd recommend is that you look to see if you can find an exploded diagram of your gun online and perhaps even an article on how to adjust the trigger on your gun. Brownell's is an online and catalog site that specializes in firearms and parts. They have the most complete collection of free exploded gun diagrams I've ever seen.

Remington model 700 (and many other models by Remington who use this trigger type) are some of the easiest triggers to adjust by turning three simple screws. My Browning A-Bolt has a single trigger adjustment screw making it extremely simple, and most of my pistols have now had a few light rubs on the sear with 1000 grit sandpaper to lighten them anywhere from 3-5lbs. The following link is an excellent resource on the internet on how to adjust Remington 700 triggers, it's the methodology I use and it's made a world of difference on my Remington rifles:

http://www.quarterbore.com/library/articles/rem700trigger.html

Ammunition

There are only two things I'd like to say about ammunition for elk hunting. The first is to make sure you are shooting the exact same brand, weight, and bullet type that you sighted your gun in with. I reload my own rounds and have played around with multiple combinations varying powder by a grain or less and seating the bullet at different depths. I have been amazed to see bullets hit up to 2 inches off by varying the powder by a few grains. Not just vertically either, I mean watching my bullets hit two inches to the left of where my gun was sighted in to hit at 100 yards. Most ammunition out there is acceptable; I've found the joy of adjusting certain aspects of a round to get groups less than a dime in diameter, but we're not talking about reloading. Buy a good brand of ammunition and stick with the exact same one.

The other aspect about ammunition is the type of bullet the cartridge is loaded with. There are many choices including Nosler partitions, soft points, hollow point, etc. Each bullet is actually designed to do something a little bit different on impact. Many premium bullets are designed to hold their shape longer before mushrooming, thereby creating a longer wound channel in the animal. This can be a bit more important when hunting game like elk as you may have to get through thick layers of fur, skin, and possibly bone before you reach the vitals. Standard bullets are usually designed to mushroom quickly which should cause a quick kill, however the premium bullets such as the Nosler partitions, Speer Trophy Bonded, Remington Core-Lokt, Winchester Fail Safe, and my new favorite, the Hornady Interbond are designed to hold together longer allowing the bullet to get deeper before expansion or fragmentation. Any of the aforementioned bullets will do the job for you however you must understand the difference and choose a bullet style for your hunting style.

If you feel strongly that you won't take a shot over 200 yards, perhaps a less expensive box of Federal soft point bullets will do the trick in 180 grain. If you're going to be shooting at longer distances though, you'll want to consider something that's specifically designed for larger game animals such as a Nosler partition or Remington Core-Lokt. These bullets usually retain 60-80 percent of their original weight up entry and then begin to mushroom into a much larger projectile. This can be important at longer ranges where the bullet will slow down considerably before hitting its target. Bullets that arrive on target too slowly have a tendency to fragment early. This could result in a shallow surface wound on an animal as tough as an elk, something you definitely don't want.

Sighting in your Rifle

I've run into a lot of folks shooting and sighting in their rifles at the local gun club, and depending on who you talk to, you'll get quite a few interesting opinions and beliefs on how to properly sight in a rifle, along with some serious BS.

Here are a few of the funnier one's I've heard in the past:

1. "Bullets rise once they leave the barrel" - Sorry, but no. Gravity is constant.

2. "Scope height doesn't matter" - You'll see later that line of sight is important as well as your cheek weld to the rifle.

3. "You need to sight your scope to shoot low at 100 yards since bullets rise" (told to me by a friend when we went to sight in his rifle, this was told to him by a popular outdoor retailer's employee)

If you really want to understand the science of the concepts, I'd highly suggest purchasing a book called "The Hunter's Guide to Ballistics" by Wayne Van Zwoll. This book is a literal treasure trove of information that is relevant to the hunter. For the purposes of general understanding, I'll summarize the concepts below. Before we begin though, there are a few concepts that you should become familiar with:

1. Point Blank; Point blank is where it all begins. It's where your scope, the bullet, and the rifle are all closest together. Because the scope is mounted higher and pointing slightly downward, the scope line of sight will cross the bullet's trajectory.

2. Mid-Range Lift; Mid-range rise is the highest point in the bullet's trajectory between the point blank range and where the bullet will finally reconnect with the scope line of sight (true zero).

3. True Zero; As the bullet falls on its natural trajectory, the scope's line of sight and the bullet's path will eventually come back together. This is true zero or just zero as most people think of it as.

4. Maximum Point Blank Range; Maximum point blank range is fairly easy to calculate. Take the distance from mid-range lift to true zero. That same distance above or below true zero will still fall well within the kill zone of an elk.

These terms are best illustrated:

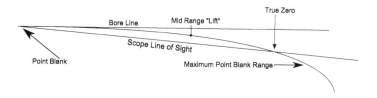

The reason a lot of people think that bullets rise is because the scope itself must be pointed downward to intersect the bullet's path. The bullet actually crosses the line once at Point

Blank, and then continues on in more of an arc causing the bullet to appear to rise. The bullet finally intersects the line of sight again at the point most of us are familiar with, which is true zero.

Now here's where things get interesting, most of the hunters I know zero their rifle for 200 yards, then compensate if the shot is shorter or longer than that. The key here is to understand where the mid-range rise and maximum point blank range fall. By understanding these two points, you'll know that you can aim dead on at a much further distance than what you've actually zeroed in at.

Let's focus on mid-range lift or rise first. During the arc of the bullet's trajectory, the bullet flies above the line of sight to some maximum before starting to fall. Let's say that the bullet flies 3" above the line of sight at 75 yards and then begins its descent. The bullet crosses the line of sight again at 200 yards (because that's how we set it) and continues then to fall below line of sight. Let's say then that the bullet drops another 3" at 275 yards. The bullet will have spanned 6" of vertical total from 75 to 275 yards, which means the bullet will hit 3" high of the center of an elk's vitals at 75 yards, and 3" low of the center of an elk's vitals at 275 yards, both of these are well within effective killing area. Now 300 yards is a pretty long shot, I don't like taking shots further than that. Armed with this information, I no longer have to adjust for bullet drop anywhere in between 75 and 300 yards, I just aim dead on.

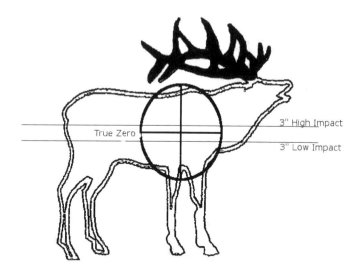

Keep in mind the factors that would effect this equation such as flatter shooting bullets will give a longer maximum point blank range (yes, feel free to use this excuse when justifying the purchase of a new gun), higher scope rings will create a steeper line of sight for the scope affecting mid-range rise. Shooting at different distances will help you determine your bullet's mid-range rise since that's a hard one to calculate, but you may want to start at 50, then move to 100 to see where they hit.

Jumpstart Chapter 2

- Bring any gear you think you might need, and even the things you don't think you'll need

- Keep your gear separated into standard which has everything you'd need regardless of the type of hunting, and then separate bins for each style of hunting (archery, rifle, muzzleloading, etc.)

- Faster and lighter bullets have less drop at longer ranges allowing for greater error in distance judgment

- Make sure you practice shooting your rifle off-hand, not just on a bench

- Get your trigger adjusted down to between 2 and 4 pounds for the best accuracy

- Make sure you are shooting the exact same brand, weight, and bullet type that you've sighted in your gun with

- Keep your knife razor sharp with a hand-held sharpener that scrapes metal off the blade, it's much faster than a stone

3

Chapter 3: Gear Opinions

Take this section for what it is, guidance in the absence of knowledge or plainly my opinion. You may agree, you may not, that's OK. The point of this book is to give you answers if you have nowhere else to turn, but keep in mind that these are my answers based on my experience. I'm not going to give you a lot of background on some of the items that follow, if you want to read all about exit pupil sizes on binoculars and the why fully coated optics are superior, there are a ton of books, magazines, and online articles that will fill you with so much knowledge that your head will explode.

Each piece of gear listed will tell you the minimum you need to know about the category and I'll give you my real life experience with using several different items. I don't get paid, I'm not sponsored by anyone, if I've found something to be quite useful or exceptionally well made, I'll tell anyone who wants to hear all about it.

Smartphone

This piece of gear has become one of the most critical tools at my disposal. Believe it or not, a smartphone can be the Swiss army knife of your hunting gear. It takes a certain level of tech savvy to become comfortable and familiar with these tools, but once you do, you won't be able to imagine going into the field without it. Granted you likely won't have cellular signal where you're hunting, but the applications available to smartphone users can make these amazingly useful tools. Even an inexpensive Android phone without service (with applications downloaded via Wi-Fi) will more than suffice. The value of the smartphone is in the applications. Below I'll list several of the applications that I've downloaded and come to rely on in the field. Most of these applications are available for or have equivalents in the Apple store.

Backcountry Navigator Pro- This app is amazing and tends to come out more than my GPS lately. Most all smartphones have a low power GPS so it will never replace my primary, however with Backcountry Navigator Pro, I can download high quality satellite images for offline use (you can't count on signal when you're in the field) and have the GPS function overlay exactly where I am on it. Additionally, you can use the same .kmz files we'll discuss later in the book within this application which will allow you to see exactly when you've entered the elk's summer/winter concentration area, or tell you exactly which game unit you're in. This is one of the few apps I use that isn't free, but for around $10, it's more than worth it.

Amazon Kindle - Although this may sound silly, I sometimes read a bit during the day if I don't want to hike back to camp. I also have several handy guides for plant identification and the like which are useful when I'm trying to identify food sources for elk.

Elk Hunting Calls – The app I use is by "Pico Brothers". It's a free and simple app that breaks down the major elk sounds (the same ones we'll cover later) and allows you to play them right there. Each year I tend to forget the nuances of the calls and I'll sit on a log before I call, hold the phone up to my ear, press the button for the call I want to make, and then reproduce what I just heard. Remember that using electronic calls is illegal for elk in most states, so only use it softly up to your ear so you can make those same calls on a manual call.

Fishing and Hunting Solunar Tables – If you happen to subscribe to the Solunar tables, these apps will show you the days and times that game activity is supposed to peak. The solunar tables are based on a study done many years ago where a scientist was able to show that fish and game activity heightened during certain times of the day based on the phase of the moon and sun. It won't keep me out of the field if it shows "poor day" for hunting, but I do tend to get a little more excited when I see it listing "excellent day".

Fungitron- If you've ever come across a mushroom in the field and wondered if it was edible, this handy little app will assist you in identifying the mushroom based on a variety of characteristics and provide information about it. It lists edible and poisonous which could be useful in a survival situation.

Evernote- I won't go too far into what Evernote is, but I keep all of my hunting notes from conversations with wardens to information from the internet organized by game management unit in Evernote. The makers of Evernote have created an app that allows you to sync this information to your phone and keep it in sync.

Shooter- If you are a fan of long range shooting and ballistics. There are many programs available that allow you to calculate the bullet drop for a given distance based on your current situation.

Sound Meter- Handy little app for bow hunters. I've used this app to try different sound deadening scenarios on my bow. The app will register the decibels of nearby sound. It's fun to add new string silencers or vibration dampening devices and see how much they actually reduce the decibels coming from your equipment.

Flashlight- Most smartphones these days have a built in flashlight app. If it doesn't, there are several great options available for free. This can be a wonderful backup if your flashlight batteries die, and can also be used as a strobe in an emergency situation.

Compass – Simple but effective. Many free compass apps are available to help show you the way in and out.

Camera- This is one of the primary uses of my smartphone in the field. Anything from capturing pictures of newly scouted areas, to posing with my kill after I have an elk down.

SAS Survival Guide- The official SAS survival guide has been converted into an application that can live on your smartphone without taking up any additional space in your pack. The SAS survival guide is chock full of information to help keep you alive in an emergency situation.

WindAlert- If you're not paying attention to the wind, it's definitely going to cut into your success in the field. This handy little app shows you the wind direction around your area. I use this one before I go out to see what the wind is normally doing in the mornings and evenings. This app requires data connectivity so it won't work once you're out in the field.

Podcast Addict – Although I don't use this in the field, many hunters don't realize the staggering number of podcasts on hunting that are currently available. If you're not familiar with a podcast, these are short recordings that anyone can do and publish to podcasting providers such as Apple iTunes. With Podcast Addict, you can search all the providers and download some great episodes that you can listen to in the car or on your way out to your hunt. I've gotten some great tips on several of these podcasts.

Remember one important thing, smartphones are battery hogs and with the screen brightness turned up and even moderate use, they won't last long. I use my phone as a backup for many of the items that I normally carry, and to augment them, but not to replace critical items. If possible, try to get a smartphone that allows the battery to be swapped out with a fresh one and get some spares. Another option is a small battery bank that you can plug your phone into. There are options that are quite small and can replenish a phone once if necessary. Larger ones over 10,000 mAh can charge a phone several times and are great for pack in trips.

Backpacks

What can I say, I love them. I have about six of them, but only use about two seriously anymore. I've upgraded over and over. Here is what I think are the most important points:

Size- Yes, size does matter. The reason I have so many is because I take the pack that's most appropriate for what I'm doing. For scouting, I have a very small pack that will hold a minimal amount of gear and my hydration bladder. For daytrips and spike camps, I have one that's much bigger.

Adjustability – Most packs worth their salt today can be adjusted to your frame. The point of most decent hunting packs is to put the weight on your hips and get it off your shoulders. One size really doesn't fit all when it comes to the larger packs, so if you're going to go big, make sure it can be adjusted to fit you well.

Storage – I tend to shy away from packs that have one giant compartment and everything ends up at the bottom. I've spent a lot of time digging through trying to find what I'm looking for in a mess of knives, gadgets and food. I bought one pack as it had something like 27 pockets. They were all tiny and hardly made it worth it so I returned it. A good pack will have a variety of storage pockets and they'll be easily accessible. There are ways to add more storage though, here's a quick tip. Most sporting goods stores sell smaller organizers that you can organize your gear in. These can be sewn into strategic areas on your pack, or attached easily using zip type plastic ties. For attaching them with plastic zip ties, heat up a flat head screwdriver so it's almost red hot, then simply melt two slots on each side of the bag about two inches apart. Run the zip ties through the slots and attach them to your pack.

Shoulder pad material – This is huge to me. Cheaper packs will end up taking their toll on your shoulders. Most good packs today have more than just a thin layer of polyester fill in the shoulder straps. This makes a world of difference when carrying a load.

So what are the two packs I use most? The first is my scouting pack which is a Badlands Hypervent series. This is a great pack for early season scouting when I know it will be hot out and all I really need are the bare essentials and water. This pack actually has stays that keep the pack off of your back and keeps a good airflow between you and your water/gear. This pack is amazing when you're hiking back at 3:00PM in August and its 85 degrees out. I hate having my clothes drenched in sweat; this pack is just the ticket. My second pack is a pack that I've fallen absolutely in love with. It's called the X-1 by Eberlestock. Glenn Eberlestock makes tactical and hunting packs and this one has some of the most well thought out features I've ever seen. I packed out over 90lbs of elk out in one trip with this pack, a total of about 2.5 miles and it was comfortable all the way given the excessive weight. It's amazingly well constructed and there's attention to detail where it matters, things like oversized loops on the zippers, and even a small hook inside the main pocket to hang your keys. The hydration pocket sits on the side of the pack and has its own compartment which keeps your water from getting on your gear should your hydration pack spring a leak. Most important to me, it has one of the most unique designs for carrying either a rifle or a bow.

I began looking for a pack with a better method of carrying a bow as my previous pack carried it way too low. This caused it to bang against my legs when walking, and made it inaccessible should I need to get it off my back quickly. I typically hike through the brush during the wee hours of the morning while it's still pitch black outside. Since I won't be shooting it while I'm walking, it makes it so wonderful to be able to secure it to the back and use your hands to move brush aside. It even comes with a quick release that you can access your bow should you ever need to make a quick shot off the trail. It carries my bow high enough to keep it comfortable and away from my legs, but not so high as to make it cumbersome when ducking under branches. The other thing I love about this back is that it has a built in full rifle scabbard that tucks away when not in use. The scabbard is large enough to accommodate a scoped rifle and cover it all the way to the comb of a rifle stock.

I've climbed many mountains with my rifle securely tucked into the scabbard and it's amazingly convenient. The rifle sits where it's reasonably accessible should you need to take a quick shot, and carries very comfortably. The pack weighs in at about 5lbs by itself, a pound or two heavier than the average day pack, but it's so versatile that I'm willing to carry a little extra weight for a pack where one size fits all. The hip belt has straps to secure extras too; it is a bit limited on pockets, so I've attached a small accessory pouch to the side where it won't interfere with my bow.

One other pack that I'd feel comfortable recommending is the Badlands Super 2200 daypack. I don't personally own one, but two of my hunting buddies do and they swear by them. Badlands make an excellent pack, you could hardly go wrong with any of their choices; however they state on their site that they sell more of this model than all of their other packs combined. That's pretty impressive.

Binoculars

So here's the part where I tell you to buy the best optics you can afford, right? Well, yes, however I'll include that I don't feel you need to spend a small fortune on optics. There are some great deals to be had out there on some excellent quality binoculars. Personally, I don't have $1500 to drop on a nice set of Swarovski's, so I have to make do with something a little less pricy. I own a pair of rubberized Steiner Bighorn 9X40 binoculars and they've served me quite well for over a decade. Even as the newer HD glass has come into play, I've sat at sunset glassing the field behind my house and could pick out detail with my Steiners that wasn't as prevalent with newer glass. They have all the important features of an excellent pair of binoculars such as fully coated lenses, waterproof, fog-proof, etc., and they set me back about $250. Recently I stumbled upon a company called Zen-Ray while doing research on optics. Zen-Ray is very popular within the bird watching forums (these people take optics seriously) and the more I read the more my interest was piqued. The consensus is that they reverse engineered a set of Swarovski binoculars and reproduced them. I can't say whether or not that is true, but I can tell you that the quality of them is amazing. My set is a 10x43 ED3 which I find to be the perfect balance of weight and field of view. At around $450, you get Swarovski function at around half the price. Brands like Steiner, Vortex, and the new Bushnell HD's offer very good quality and are reasonably priced. I wouldn't recommend skimping too heavily on optics though, if you're spending less than a couple of hundred dollars, it's likely that the manufacturer is skimping somewhere and that typically equates to strain on your eyes

The only other factor to mention is size. Too large and they're a pain to carry, too small and they won't give you the field of view that you need to properly glass an area. If you have money to burn, consider buying a pair of 10x42 and something smaller like an 8x32. The last thing I'll say on binoculars is no matter how much you spend, the straps they give you always seem to be sub-standard. There are many brands of binocular harnesses out there for around $30. I just got one this last season and I can't even begin to tell you the difference it made. I can vividly remember the discomfort from my old binocular strap, this year, I hardly even knew they were there. Treat yourself; you'll be glad you did.

Spotting scopes

I consider spotting scopes an accessory for the trophy hunter, but not a necessity for me. Don't get me wrong, I own one. It's an Alpen and this year it helped me determine the sex of an antelope at 427 yards before making the shot. There's no way I could have been sure with a pair of binoculars. Since purchasing my spotting scope, I've taken it out a whopping one time when elk hunting. Why? Because it's big, bulky, and I'm not particularly concerned about antler size. I'm a meat hunter and will take the first legal animal that comes my way. All I really have to do is to be able to see the fact that it is an elk and I'm golden. If you're after the trophy of a lifetime, by all means, buy one, but for the casual elk hunter where even a 5 point is a well-earned trophy, you'll appreciate the extra space and less weight in your pack. If you do decide that you absolutely have to have one, most of the information in the binoculars section is relevant to spotting scopes as well. If you get one with too little power magnification, it won't offer much over a decent set of binoculars. If you get a cheaper one, I wouldn't count on using it for very long before the lower quality optics begin to take their toll on your eyes. I'd suggest somewhere between 24 and 36 power at maximum zoom, and as a general rule, weight relates to quality so see if you can handle the brand you're interested in before you buy it. Also, spotting scopes that offer angled eye pieces are much easier to use when scanning terrain from a vantage point in the woods, straight eye pieces are easier when glassing from a vehicle.

GPS

I consider myself a semi-expert here as I've owned about five of them. That may not be too many to some, but it's enough for me to know where certain features have made a difference. Later on we're going to get into virtual scouting and using a computer to assist you in locating better than average hunting spots. Don't worry if you're not a computer guy, we'll keep it simple and build on that. I'm a bit of a gadget freak and am very comfortable with computers so when I went to purchase my last GPS, I sought one with a few particular features that have really paid dividends.

I currently use a Garmin Oregon 550. It's not the only GPS that can do what I'm about to describe, but it does it does everything well, it integrates with many third party utilities, and the price was reasonable. The Garmin Oregon has the ability to communicate natively with Google Earth and upload actual aerial photographs of the terrain that I'll be hunting. One trick I've been able to perform with this particular unit is the ability to outline forest boundaries and private land boundaries in Google Earth, and then actually import them into my GPS. When you're in the field, you can switch on this layer and easily assess whether or not you're getting close to private property or somewhere else you shouldn't be. A few other nice features include a three axis compass so it doesn't "reset" the direction when you put your arms at your side, and it has a built in camera which you can use to associate pictures with areas you've scouted and marked.

Radio

Most of the radios today are pretty standard. Some of them tout a 30 mile range even. Well, maybe on perfectly flat land with no obstructions, but that probably won't be the range you'll get. You're likely to get only a few miles, but that should be enough to stay in touch with your hunting party while you're splitting up or asking for help once your elk is down. Try to get a model with the greatest possible range and make sure it has a vibrate mode. There's nothing worse than hearing that annoying beep of a walkie talkie after trying so hard to ensure that you've been completely silent. Many radios also have earpieces that allow you to listen and talk without touching the unit. This is a very nice feature to have as well. Lastly, I'd try to get the smallest unit you can find and use that as a tie breaker if there are two you're considering.

Amplified Hearing Aids

I don't use one of these, I've owned one and although it did work well regarding amplifying the sounds I heard, the problem is it amplifies ALL the sounds you hear, mostly the ones closest to you. The clothing I wear is pretty quiet, especially when I'm bow hunting. Even with the quietest of fabrics, my movements always seemed to fill my ears with the most annoying rustling, even when only turning my head. I've heard about 75% of the elk I've encountered before I ever saw them, and I have no idea how many I didn't see because I didn't hear them. If your hearing is good, just learn to get quiet and listen for the smallest sounds of leaves crunching or squirrels chattering alarms nearby, these telltale signs will give you the edge you need without an expensive hearing aid.

Rangefinder

This is an essential tool as far as I'm concerned. Ranging objects accurately is extremely difficult and judging range uphill, downhill, and at long distances is even more challenging. Newer range finders have an excellent built in function that compensates for angle when you're ranging uphill or downhill which can be a lifesaver for bow hunters. Regardless of the range the company claims it goes, get the longest distance you can. I had a 400 yard rangefinder from Nikon that was good to about 250 yards in reality. I now have an 800 yard rangefinder which is good to about 600 yards in reality. Beyond that, I get spotty readings if I get a reading at all. 600 yards is longer than I'll ever take a shot at, so I'm hoping my current rangefinder lasts a long time.

Treestands

Yes indeed, I've hunted elk for years out of a treestand in Colorado. Most hunters associate treestands with hunting for Whitetails out east, but depending on the spot that I'm hunting and the access, hunting out of a treestand gives the hunter a unique advantage when it comes to sight and smell, two of the factors that give away a hunter the majority of the time. I've begun to shy away from treestands a bit as I find myself packing in farther; however it's hard to beat the advantage they offer if you know the area is a consistent elk crossing. The only area I'll take my treestand anymore is at the end of a 2 mile trail that opens into a meadow where elk tend to cross during archery season. Getting the treestand to your spot is usually the most difficult part, so when we hunt this area, we use a big game cart and load it up with our treestands, extra water, and harnesses and take it up the mountain ahead of time. We have a favorite spot nearby that we stash our cart and treestands at so we can go up and down the mountain afterwards with only our packs. If I'm not using the cart, I typically won't use the treestand either as I'm not going to carry up both a treestand and a pack.

Most treestands on the market or either fixed or climbing in design. I prefer the climbing as I can easily change angles or even locations however we've found that the straps and padded seats make irresistible chew toys for the local squirrels if you leave them out. I've traded in a few models to get the lightest one I could find that was sturdy as well. Anything that you'll have to transport, even if it's only for a short distance, should be less than 20lbs. You don't need a treestand to hunt elk so if you prefer not to purchase one that's fine. We'll discuss a few tactics later to help minimize your movement and if you're keeping clean and hunting the wind, you should do well on the ground.

Blinds

Blinds are a useful tool but also bulky. As with tree-stands, I find myself not wanting to lug something that heavy up the hill unless I'm taking a load up on my big game cart. Double bull blinds are about the best you can get, but they're bulky and heavy. I have a smaller blind made with non-reflective fabric that has enough room for me to sit comfortably and draw back my bow, and enough mesh windows that I can easily see in all directions. I typically camouflage my blind with branches that I've cut away or find laying on the forest floor to break up the outline. I've been busted countless times by making the smallest of movements when elk are near, typically trying to get a better look at which way they're coming when obstructed by a branch or tree. You'll note that I'm speaking mostly in terms of archery here where the animals will be close and typically either looking for me from my calls, or passing by a well-used trail. I've never taken my blind during rifle season, I think it would be more of a hindrance as even the best of blinds will obstruct your long range view.

61

Blinds do help tremendously if you're fidgety and just can't quite keep still. If you are going to buy a blind, just remember a few things. First, make sure you want to carry that much weight and bulk up the mountain. Second, make sure that it's big enough to accommodate drawing back a bow. I found out the hard way that having too small of a blind makes hunting quite difficult.

Flashlights/headlamps

My hunting buddies used to make me walk the trail behind them because my light was so bright. This was actually a good thing as they wanted me there so they could see the trail! I used a 1 watt Browning Black Ice headlamp with a band that goes around your head or hat. The light was great, except for one thing. It used proprietary type camera batteries that were very expensive and not interchangeable with other items. I still have that unit but its collecting dust in after my purchase of a $10 LED headlamp at Wal-Mart that takes AAA batteries. The LED headlamps throw out a ton of light and I can change out the batteries cheaply every year to ensure that I have plenty of light for my trips up the mountain.

Knives

When I was about 21, I asked for a set of high quality knives for my birthday. I love to cook and was in the food service field at the time, so having a good set of knives made sense. The guys I worked with used an industrial tri-stone to sharpen their knives and I eventually acquired one of those too. The reason I'm going into all of this is because after the first year or so of using the tri-stone, I put it away and began using a small sharpener with two carbide type edges that literally scrapes metal off the blade to get an edge. When I first saw the small spirals of metal coming off my prized knives I was horrified. However the newness of my knives soon wore off and I found that the practical function of having razor sharp knives in an instant won out. Twenty years later, these knives are still in use and show very little sign of becoming smaller as I had worried about.

I do love good knives, but you'll find a folding Gerber in my pack now that I sharpen multiple times with a smaller sharpener of the same type I mentioned above. I'd rather spend $30 every few years or so and have a decent knife that I can keep razor sharp in the field (something that's tough to do when dressing a whole elk) with a few passes across a sharpener every 20-30 minutes. More expensive knives use harder metals and typically hold an edge longer, but you have to know how to sharpen them right and even then, elk are tough and you'll be amazed how quickly their hide and bone can dull even the best knife.

A few key features to look for are brightly colored knives as they seem to "disappear" multiple times during the process of field dressing an elk, and a non-slip type rubber checkering to give you a firm grip when the knife gets covered in blood.

Boots

There are a few items that you'll find that I deem unnec-essary, or I'll recommend that you don't spend a ton of money on, boots aren't on that list. I strongly suggest that you don't buy boots off the internet unless you have tried them on in a store or are purchasing a pair that you've owned and loved before. The best boots I've owned haven't had a break in period; they were comfortable from day one. I own about six pairs, but honestly use two. The first is a pair of lighter weight boots with 400 grams of Thinsulate built into them. These are the boots I use when scout-ing and archery hunting as they'll keep my feet warm enough during the cool mornings and not so hot that my feet sweat while hiking during the day. I found a pair that zip down on the sides and also tie making them snug on my feet but easy to get off once back at camp.

My second pair has a full 1000 grams of Thinsulate and these puppies are as waterproof as boots can get. There's nothing worse than cold feet when you're elk hunting during third season with blowing winds and 12 inches of snow. Do yourself a favor, if your feet are too warm, you'll be uncomfortable, if your feet are too cold, you'll be miserable. Remember that one of the primary goals of this books is to keep you hunting longer and given that, boots are not an area to skimp on. There's nothing worse than low quality boots that cause hot spots or calluses in the field. Plan on spending $200-300 dollars on a good pair of boots such as Lowa, Meindle, Schnee's or Kentrek. They'll last you for years and you'll find your ability to stay out longer and hike further greatly enhanced.

Socks

Yes, an entire section dedicated to socks, that's how important I think they are. Outside of a good pair of boots, socks are what are going to keep you going during the long hikes. They also keep your feet warm and dry when your feet get wet from sweat or moisture, and keep blisters from forming on your feet when walking up and down hills. If you can only afford a few good pairs of socks, don't worry about wearing them several times on your hunt. If you buy a premium quality wool sock such as smartwool socks, they'll wick moisture away from your feet and keep foot odor from forming. They'll cushion your feet and you'll be able to do twice the hiking you could with a pair of cotton socks or the cheap wool socks of lower quality.

Actually being out in the field and covering a lot of ground has more to do with your success than most gadgets you'll buy for hunting. As trivial as it may seem, excellent quality socks will keep you out there longer and help you go farther, so save the money you were going to spend on that combination super elk bugle/vacuum hose extension and buy some good socks, you'll thank yourself later.

Camouflage

My basement is literally overflowing with it. I have camo clothing for all seasons and every time I see more on sale, I buy it. I now know what sits on my shelves untouched, what always goes in my bag, and what's given me away. What sits on my shelves are the heavy duty coveralls that I've purchased. I bought them with the intention of using them for elk hunting, but they are just too restrictive. They have one speed when it comes to warmth, and that's super-warm. This may seem like a good thing, but really dressing in layers is the way to go. I've been snowed on in the mountains in early September, and baked in the sun in mid-October. I've frozen my butt off as the sun began to peek over the horizon and move the air currents causing the temperature to temporarily drop 15 degrees only to be roasting an hour later once the winds died down and the sun was beating down on my back.

Buying multiple layers will allow you to add or subtract clothing as you need it and make sure you're comfortable throughout the day. Also remember that only your outer layer needs to be camouflage, I typically bring a warm sweatshirt for a layer underneath should it get cold. The elk don't see it under my camo shirt that's over it, so I don't care whether or not it's camo. Regarding the camouflage pattern, most of them will do. I think we've gotten a little carried away with the whole designer camo thing. Camouflage is meant to break up your outline. This is important as the wrong kind of camo can actually be more detrimental than helpful.

Jumpstart Elk Hunting

Years ago I purchased quite a lot of Mossy Oak Breakup camouflage clothing. This pattern is particularly dark and didn't match the shades of the area I hunted in which was mostly aspen and pine. In a treestand, I was a large dark blob sitting there that looked amazingly out of place. Buy whatever floats your boat, but try to match the shades of the camo over anything else. Some of my favorite camo now are the pieces I purchased for duck hunting with a wetlands style pattern. It breaks up my outline really well in both the areas I elk hunt and the areas I duck and goose hunt. The lighter colors of the wetlands, marsh, or even camo patterns similar to brush make excellent dual purpose camouflage. There are even region specific patterns to match conifer and aspen trees in both the spring and fall. You can build up quite a collection of camouflage so try to maximize your hunting dollars.

Game Cameras

I almost left this one out, but remembered how important these devices have been to my success in the past. I bought a few of them many years ago and set them up during scouting trips. The areas I covered were areas that I knew held elk and I wanted to see what was "hanging around" and when. It's fun and exciting to pull these down and see all the activity that has gone on, nothing gets my blood pumping more than seeing a six point monster feeding right across my hunting spot. Recently I purchased a few more and set them up in an area that looked absolutely perfect. I was 100% convinced that the elk would be traveling through this one hub of trails. Three weeks later I pulled down my camera only to find hundreds of pictures of cows (dairy kind) and a few shots of a rancher riding his horse by. This trail had it all and I would have surely hunted there the following year. Instead, I hunted a nearby trail without domestic activity that proved much more successful.

If you're going to get a few, get as many megapixels as you can afford (no need to spend more than $100 each) and find units that are smaller and take AA batteries instead of C or D sized. When you head up to plant four or five of them, having a smaller form factor will make a big difference when lugging them around

I wouldn't worry much about them being stolen either, I have a hard enough time finding these things when I know where they are! Just make sure you mark your GPS with the position the moment you put it up. I forgot to do this once, and even though I knew "exactly" where the camera was, it took me about 20 minutes of searching to find it.

In the last year, several manufacturers have come out with "Plot watcher" type cameras that take a picture at set intervals (usually between 10 seconds and 5 minutes) regardless of whether or not it detects motion. I became a huge fan of these as many meadows that I hunt are large and a single camera can watch the entire area. The images stitch together to create a movie for rapid analysis so you don't have to worry about viewing thousands of images individually. If you purchase Lithium batteries, you'll likely get about 14 days of footage at one minute intervals. 4GB cards are more than adequate as my batteries have run out long before my space has on the storage drive.

Miscellaneous

The following is a brief rundown of items that you may find useful and some tips on using them effectively where appropriate:

Small pack saw – Especially when bow hunting, you want to make sure you have clear shooting lanes for all trails and areas where you think elk may come out of. A small pocket saw will make quick work of branches that sit between you and a possible shot.

Pillow cases – Yep, pillow cases. The cheap white ones they sell at Wal-Mart with zippers on them are about the best meat bags I've found to date. They're tough and will let the meat breathe a bit. Save those mesh bags for meat quarters hanging in camp if you choose to go that way.

Plastic drop cloth – A small cheap plastic drop cloth from the hardware store comes in very handy when field dressing your kill. There's nothing worse than picking bits of dirt and pine needles out of your meat once you get home, this will save you a whole lot of headache. Get the thicker plastic sheets and cut them in half as the thinner sheets will rip easily.

Nitrile gloves – These gloves are very similar to the thin latex gloves they sell in hardware stores, but the Nitrile versions are much more durable. Don't feel like a sissy for using them either, it's not so much about not wanting to touch blood, but after you get done field dressing or boning an elk, your hands will be coated with dried blood. These gloves will keep you from having to scrape the blood off of your fingernails.

Calls

I've saved this one for last as it's a hard topic to give clear direction on. There are so many types of calls on the market and everyone has one that they swear by. I'll give you some general advice regarding choosing a call that's right for you. Mostly, your choice in calls should reflect the realities of how much you'll practice with it. Be honest with yourself on this. I have a box full of elk tubes and every kind of cow call imaginable along with some diaphragm calls mixed in. I've never found the time to practice enough given my work schedule to master most any of the bugles to where I could sound remotely like a bull. I also have a small palette and struggled for years trying to learn to use diaphragm calls unsuccessfully.

The closest I've come is with the Primo's brand sonic dome mini's that actually fit in the roof of my mouth, but I still can't get out a good bull squeal or bugle with them. The only call I feel I can blow and even begin to sound like a bull is Wayne Carlton's Mac Daddy call which sounds very good considering that everything is done internally using pressure and a simulated tongue on a diaphragm call inside a housing.

I find the bite and blow cow calls such as Wayne Carlton's Lonesome Cow call to be the easiest for a beginner without sounding awful, and other styles such as Primo's "I maka da bull crazy" call can be mastered with a little practice. Several call

70

manufacturers also make "push" calls where all the user has to do is to push in on a rubber bulb and it will make a soft mew. You're a bit limited in what you can do with them, but they're easy and very effective (I can attest). I'm a huge fan of the "Hoochie Mama" by Primo's calls. Having both bite and blow calls and push calls can be very effective when you're trying to sound like more than one elk. I keep one in my mouth and a push call either in my pocket or attached to my belt loop. Not only can I sound like more than one elk, I can talk over one with the other as elk often do when feeding in a meadow. Cow calls are hard (but not impossible) to mess up too terribly, so experiment if you can, but if not, take it easy one yourself and get something you'll realistically be able to use and be effective with.

Elk Hunting Checklist

Below you'll find my elk hunting checklist. I print this off every year when packing for my trip to ensure I don't forget anything. Remember, if you bought it, bring it. Also, you'll find each time you head out in the field, you'll probably think, "wow, it would be nice if I had...." When you get home, add these items to the list and you'll eventually build a custom list that suits you perfectly. Some of the items in this list are optional, some may vary based upon the season you're hunting, the type of trip you're taking, or the party you're hunting with.

Elk Hunting Checklist

Camp Necessities

- Tent or Sleeping quarters
- Cook stove
- Lantern
- Heating stove (optional) & Wood for Stove
- Sleeping bag(s), Sleeping Pad, Pillow
- Camping Cot
- Sponges
- Utensils (Cooking and Eating)
- Pots and Pans
- Coffee maker and coffee
- Plates and mugs
- Shower Enclosure & Shower Kit
- BBQ Grill
- Charcoal
- Foil
- Cooking oil/PAM
- Tarp
- Bungee Cords
- Gear Tent
- Water jug
- Axe/Saw
- Scent-free deodorant, soap, shampoo
- Toilet Paper
- Paper towels
- Large "Game" cooler

Hunting Equipment

- Hunting License
- Weapon
- Ammunition
- Release if bowhunting
- Broadheads if bowhunting
- Rangefinder
- Knives
- Knife Sharpener
- Game bags
- Bone Saw
- Latex Gloves
- Binoculars
- Compass
- GPS
- 1 roll of orange tape
- Face Paint
- Headlight and small flashlight
- 2-way Radio
- Backpack
- Treestand (Optional)
- Game Cart (Optional)
- Zip ties
- 1 Bottle of Elk Scent
- 1 Bottle of Scent Eliminator
- Elk Calls
- Hand-Warmers
- First Aid/Survival Kit
- Fresh batteries (AA & AAA)
- Phone battery pack

- Medium Food cooler
- Alarm Clock
- Chair(s)
- Tarp
- Rope
- Cloth Towels
- Portable Table
- Camera
- Targets
- Bug Spray

Food
- Camp Food
- Pack Food
- Water

Things to do:
- Check Batteries
- Check weapon (scope tight on rifle, moving parts ok on bow)
- Tell someone where you're going to be

- Maps
- Hydration Pack

Clothing
- Hunting Boots
- Regular Tennis Shoes
- Socks for (1 per day +2 spare)
- 1 Camo Shirt per day
- 1 Camo Pant per Day
- 1 Camo Jacket
- 1 Camp Sweatshirt
- 1 Camp Shorts
- 2-3 sets Street Clothing
- 2-3 Sets Long Johns
- 1 Set Rain Gear
- 1 Set Gaitors
- Hunting Cap (Radar)
- Hunting Cap (Cold Weather)
- Orange Vest
- 1 or 2 pair Warm Gloves
- Camo Belt
- Underwear (1 per day)
- Camo face mask

Download this list at
http://www.coloradohunters.net

Jumpstart Chapter 3

- Purchase and use equipment that take the same size batteries and only standard (AA, AAA, etc.) type
- Get a good knife sharpener, preferably the carbide type to keep your knife razor sharp
- Bring two pairs of boots, one for warmer weather, one for colder
- Buy excellent quality socks, they'll make the difference
- Camouflage patterns need to match the shade of the terrain you're hunting, not necessarily the exact foliage
- Buy layering type clothes, nothing too heavy, nothing too light
- Use your elk hunting checklist every year, add to it as soon as possible once you return

Chapter 4: Critical Information about Elk

Just like anything else in life, the more you know about a subject the better prepared you are. Understanding elk and their motivations is critical to increasing your odds of success in the field. In a later chapter, we'll discuss methodologies for finding elk on maps, on the computer, and out in the field so it will be helpful to have a solid understanding of why we're eliminating certain areas and why we're targeting other areas for further exploration. If you've elk hunted before, then you've certainly been in the situation of wondering where the elk are when they aren't in the area you're hunting. The ability to dissect an area and analyze it based on knowledge about elk behavior and preferences will help tremendously in knowing whether you should stick with an area or move on, and even help identify where to move on to.

A Day in the Life of an Elk

Elk don't live very complicated lives. You don't need to be a Psychologist to figure out what motivates an elk, it's pretty simple. Food, water, safety, breeding, and comfort are the five biggest factors in figuring out what the elk will be up to and where they might be. Let's look at each factor one at a time to further understand the finer points of these motivating factors.

Food – Elk need to eat, as a matter of fact, they need to eat quite a bit to sustain their large size. The average elk will eat about three pounds of food per day per 100 pounds of body weight. When you think about the weight of grasses being plucked from the meadows or browse from in the trees, you'll understand that elk are going to need a lot of time to get the amount of food they need to survive. Elk do have preferences when it comes to food, the local Wildlife Biologist can be helpful in understanding the kinds of food that elk will sustain themselves with, however if you delve into elk biology, you'll find quite a long list of grasses, browse, berries and the like that elk will eat to survive. Being able to identify all of these is a task better suited for biology majors so I won't go too far into this exhaustive list. Just understand that elk need food and depending on the time of year, they'll be able to find it relatively easily. The more important factors to understand when looking at an elk's eating habits are how much food an elk requires. This should help you understand how long and how often they'll feed, and how an elk processes the food that it eats.

Elk feel safest when it's quiet and they can tune into the environment around them. That's not the case when they're pulling up grasses with their teeth, chewing, and putting their heads down to get their next bite. Elk are ungulates and have four stomachs, much like a domestic cow. Elk will eat enough to fill up chambers within their stomach and later regurgitate their food to further chew and process it for their digestive system. This is the time elk will bed down in a safe spot to chew their cud and begin making room to fill up again at their next feeding later in the evening.

The activity of eating by itself takes up a goodly portion of an elk's day, especially during the fall months as an elk begins to prepare for limited food availability in winter. As for the bulls, the months prior to the rut will have the bull feeding more and on better quality forage to build up the fat stores required to sustain him through the chasing, fighting and herding of cows he'll be doing during the rut.

Water – This one should be pretty easy to understand, we know all living creatures need water. Elk can find sources of water all over the forest so just because you don't see a stream cutting through an area doesn't mean that there's no water there. Elk will get water from ponds, streams, springs, pools left from melted snow, and even from the dew left behind on the leaves in the morning. Obviously the safer they feel at a watering hole the better, but take note the next time you're out in the field of how many little trickling brooks and tiny seeping springs you find as you scout. If there are water sources in the area, elk will use them and it's not always as easy as finding a stream cutting through an area when trying to locate the elk.

Safety – This is a big one. Elk aren't just hunted by humans; they're prey to many other predators in the forest such as coyotes, wolves, mountain lions, etc. If elk seem skittish in general, it's for good reason as they must constantly have their guard up. Elk understand where they're safer and where they're more at risk. I'm convinced it has to do with behaviors that are passed down as calves notice that mom gets a little more edgy when out in the open or when human activity levels pick up prior to most hunting seasons. As I mentioned earlier, elk need to spend a good amount of time feeding, and where is the best feed going to be? It will be in areas that have all the requirements for things to grow which are soil, water, and most importantly, sunlight. This is why you'll see elk feeding in open meadows versus in thick black timber. Simply put, the best feed is going to grow in some of the least safe areas. So what's an elk to do? The answer is simply to feed in areas that offer the best source of food but where safety is also a mere jump away. This is why elk will feed on the edges of meadows more often than in the middle as they know that the safety of the thick timber is only a few steps off. Many of the smaller "pockets" you'll find, where small meadows only a few hundred yards wide are surrounded by tall timber, are favorite elk grounds as they'll feel safer feeding in them.

Wildlife biologists refer to areas where different types of environments meet as edges. Studies have shown that there are more animals per square foot in edges than in any other type of terrain. This is an important fact to keep in mind when elk hunting during feeding hours as these are likely spots to find elk.

Once finished feeding, elk want to go somewhere safe to process their food. Those thick areas of black forest which are so difficult for humans to navigate through offer excellent protection and privacy for elk as they regurgitate their food. These are referred to as bedding areas are the spots elk are most likely to haunt during the afternoons prior to their feeding times. Finally, it doesn't take elk long to figure out where they get shot at and where they don't. It really comes down to the intrusion of humans on their areas more than bullets whizzing by their heads. Elk associate humans with danger and when humans begin intruding, driving ATVs, slamming doors, and walking through their areas, they'll go either to the thickest of black timber or the closest private land they can find where they can go about their business undisturbed.

Breeding – Well, if you're a guy reading this book, I don't have to tell you that females can make us do stupid things. Elk are no different and the breeding season presents an opportunity for bulls to round up a harem of cows and hopefully keep them until he's bred them all. Whether you realize it or not, organisms are hard-wired to keep their gene pool going. Scientific debate still goes on regarding whether it's at the level of the organism itself, or all the way down to the cell, but regardless there's a reason why men are so interested in sex, plainly and simply, it's genetically pre-programmed into us. Bull elk go a little crazy come mid-September (or whenever the rut may occur in your area) and their whole job in life is to round up as many cows as they can to breed.

Now this isn't as simple as it sounds. The cows are also hard-wired to ensure their offspring have the greatest chance for survival. Their job is to get "herded" by the biggest, most genetically perfect specimen they can find to ensure their calf will be born healthy, survive, and carry on their gene pool as well. Bulls will spend most of their time trying to herd other cows, protecting what they have, and breeding the cows when they come into estrus (a short period of time, usually less than 24 hours).

Some younger cows may come into estrus later, or cows that didn't have the opportunity to be bred may enter a second estrus cycle in the third week of the rut. Important information to note as we'll discover later. Also keep in mind what's on the bull's mind. Sex, that's all. Not fighting, not keeping to his daily patterns, all he's thinking about is breeding cows, keeping his cows, and getting more cows where the risk doesn't involve losing what he's got. A bull typically won't go running into another bull's challenge unless that bull poses an immediate threat to the other bull's interests. It's much easier and safer for a bull to just herd up his cows and take them up the mountain versus getting into an altercation.

Herd bulls, the "perfect" specimens that all the ladies want to be with are especially reluctant to leave as picking up a cow or two isn't worth the risk of a pesky satellite bull coming in and trying to make off with one of his cows. Apologies to anyone who might take offense to this, but if you're after a bull, then you need to think like a man. If you had a bunch of women surrounding you, would you be interested in running off to chase down one more or fighting some guy yelling from across the bar that he's going to kick your butt? Myself, I'd take my ladies and go, but hey, I'm a lover, not a fighter.

Comfort – This is one aspect of elk hunting that most hunting books don't cover, yet it's an extremely important motivating factor for elk. Elk are just like any other creature; we all want to be as comfortable as possible. Elk are sturdy animals that are made to survive in harsh conditions. They must be able to endure freezing cold temperatures and wind that would send lesser animals to their deaths. Their coats are excellent insulators and their hides are very thick. Unfortunately for elk though, this works against them in the summer months of archery season as they lack an extensive sweat gland system to keep cool. The best elk can do is to find a cooler "micro-climate" where the heat is bearable. Many books refer to north and east facing slopes during summer for a reason. Next time you're in the mountains hiking in the heat, I guarantee you that you'll find the closest north or east facing slope in which to take a break. You'll be much cooler in the shade of the trees than on the south or west facing slopes where the sun is beating down. Elk also have preferences related to degree of slope and mountain zones.

Studies cited in an outstanding book called Elk of North America (Thomas & Toweill, 1982) found that "nearly 60 percent of all elk use was on slopes less than 18 percent", and that "About half of all elk use was in the 0-18 percent slope class during spring and autumn, whereas more than two-thirds of summer and winter use was in this class." Studies also cited that "elk generally preferred upper, middle, and lower slopes, in that order." Perhaps this has more to do with safety than comfort as elk are notorious for watching below them while they bed, or maybe the top third of the mountain is cooler, regardless, that's what they like.

Other interesting snippets from Elk of North America regarding habitat include the following:

- "Elk tend to prefer upper slopes regardless of the season"
- "In winter, elk prefer upper south-facing slopes that are the first to become bare of snow"
- "Many investigators have reported that elk prefer southern to southwestern exposures in winter and spring"
- "South facing slopes are seldom selected in the summer"
- "elk preferred northeastern exposures during the summer"
- "Thermal forest cover on upper north facing slopes provides the coolest habitat during summer and the most succulent, high quality forage into autumn months"
- "...found that elk selected bedding sites that aided body temperature control, hence energy conservation. More than 80 percent of all bedding sites were associated with 'timber clumps' on the upper slopes"
- "During cold periods, day beds were on south-facing exposures of timber clumps and night beds were on north-facing exposures."
- "Older and more developed forest stands with 'natural pruning' of lower branches permit wind movement"..."This provides elk with shade, radiation, and cooling wind action as well as good visibility"

All of these points should convince you that elk aren't creatures of habit, they're creatures of comfort. Just as you'll see all the shady spots at the park taken first by happy picnickers, elk will utilize areas that aid their comfort level as dictated by the season. So let's recap for a minute. Think about all of the facts we just went over. Now we know all kinds of facts that about the motivating factors of elk. Putting this together can easily lead to, or eliminate large sections of land when planning your hunt. Simply put, your best chances for success during the summer, for example, are in areas where elevations are higher, with northeastern facing slopes of about 18 percent or less, in the upper third of the mountain, where mature timber stands are close to grassy meadows and little human activity. Couple this kind of knowledge with some of the factors we'll cover later regarding terrain features and preferences and you'll be on your way to systematically dissecting an area to identify the highest odds areas for filling your tag.

The Call of the Wild, Elk Language

The last aspect of elk that we'll touch on is the language of elk. Elk do in fact communicate and the different sounds they make can mean different things. I'll quote Paul Medel (AKA Elk Nut) when he says that you have to "make sense" when you talk to elk otherwise they'll know something's not quite right or react in a way you don't want them to. Paul sells an excellent set of instructional DVDs that go into depth on elk and elk calling so if you really want to understand and more importantly hear all the different nuances of elk language, you may wish to consider buying his

CD or DVD sets at http://www.elknut.com. Commonly though most people associate elk calls with the bugles of bulls and the mews of cows. Those bugles sure do sound beautiful and I can't help but get jealous every time I hear a well-practiced caller belt out a melodic bugle, something I still haven't been able to do.

Bulls bugle for several reasons, to attract cows, to determine the location of other bulls, and to warn other bulls that they have a claim on that area. As a beginner elk hunter, I'll warn you off of going out into the field and using a bugle. Bugles are hard to master and you'll likely chase more elk out of the area than call them in as most bulls aren't looking for a fight unless you're right in their back yard. I've heard hundreds of hunters in the forest blowing on their bugles, trying their best to imitate what they heard on last week's show on elk hunting. It's good in theory, but public land bulls aren't stupid and it takes a lot to get one over on them.

My personal favorite is cow calls. I've had so much success calling in bulls and cows with all types of cow calls that I hardly use anything else. It is important though to understand a few aspects of cow calling so you can create a "scenario" that makes sense to the elk. Each time you set out to call, you should have an idea in mind of the exact scenario you're trying to recreate and how that might actually sound. Here are a few examples of different scenarios and what types of calling you might need to do:

- A relaxed herd feeding – This scenario requires the use of multiple calls used at once. It's easiest with a buddy, however you can do it alone. When a herd is relaxed and feeding, cows will mew softly to tell the rest of the herd where they are and that all is well. The mew is a short, one second sound that goes eeeeow with the eeee part being of higher pitch and the "ow" part dropping off a bit. My absolute favorite call for making these sounds is Wayne Carlton's lonesome cow call. It's a bite and blow call that makes it very easy to use and the sounds are almost perfect compared to the herds I've listened to in the woods. A good call to compliment that call and give the single hunter the ability to sound like multiple elk is the Hootchie Mama elk call which uses a push bulb like a squeak toy to make excellent mews. A few mews from the mouth, a response from the bulb, a few seconds of silence, then a single mew from the bulb, a response from the mouth, etc.. Mix it up a bit and you'll sound just like a small herd of elk comfortably feeding in meadow. Perhaps not the best sound to use in black timber though as elk wouldn't be feeding in there based on what we know from learning about elk biology.

- The lost cow – This is my absolute favorite and one that works year round. Elk are herd animals, they find safety in numbers and don't like being alone, especially the cows. When you blow a lost cow call, cows will typically come running, even crashing, to help their lost compatriot. I've had more elk come through the timber like a freight train to this call, it's exciting so be ready! Lost cow calls are similar to a mew, but longer and a bit more panicked. Use emotion when you call, get into character. The call itself is about 2 seconds in duration and makes a similar eeeeeeeeeooooowwww sound. I do them a little faster and try to sound a little worried such as eeeeeeeeoooowwww eeeeeeeoooowwww, eeeeowww, eeeeeeeeeeoooowwww and repeat about every 15 minutes or so in my hunting spot. I was so shook up the first time I did this and a cow with two 5 point bulls came barreling through the aspens and stopped 30 yards in front of me staring right at me. Obviously this call would work well in the thicker timber where elk might get separated from each other, but getting lost can happen anywhere so practice this one and you'll be amazed how well it works.

- The Satellite and the reluctant cow- This is a fun scenario to do with a buddy, but you can do it by yourself if you work quickly. When a bull collects all his cows, other bulls known as satellite bulls will hang out along the fringes of the bull's area waiting for an opportunity to steal a cow to breed. Remember that cows don't want to be bred by a lesser bull, so they'll put up a fuss if a smaller satellite bull is hooking them with his antlers and trying to lead her away. Hooking is what bulls do to cows by turning their heads and jabbing their antlers into the cow's body to force her back into or away from the herd. Think for a second about what that might sound like. The cow would whine with high pitched mews, a little desperate as she doesn't want to go willingly. The satellite bull may let out a squeal or grunt to try to help convince her that this is for her own good. A nearby bull may well seize this opportunity to come in a chase the other bull off and take the cow for himself. You can see how this would make sense, even in human terms. Most guys can picture seeing a beautiful young lady being dragged out of a bar against her will and coming to the rescue (in the hopes of course of taking her willingly out of the bar later).

- The estrus/late estrus cow – This one is a little more challenging and much less frequently heard on elk hunting dvds and shows. When cow elk are ready to be bred, they only have a short period of time and they know it. They'll sometimes whine like the dickens to get the attention they are looking for. This is another scenario where timing is everything. It wouldn't make much sense to an elk to hear a cow giving an estrus whine in the winter, however the week the rut kicks into full gear in your area and about three weeks afterwards could prove deadly. Estrus whines are literally a cow whining with a very nasally pitch, demanding attention as would a spoiled child. The Primos hyper lip single and the woodswise estrus cow call both make that excellent nasally tone. Imagine a cow going eeeeeeoowweeeeeeoooooowww eeeeeeoooooow, eeee-ow in a constant fluctuating tone, demanding that someone come and pay attention to her.

Jumpstart Chapter 4

- Food, water, safety, breeding, and comfort are the five most important factors in determining where the elk will be
- Elk spend a lot of time feeding, and they do it several times during the day
- Elk feed in areas that have the best forage, these will typically be meadows where sunlight and moisture allows for growth and nearby timber allows for safety
- Studies have shown that there are more animals in areas were two or more types of terrain meet (edges) than any single type of terrain
- Elk are most likely to be in thick timbered bedding areas in the earlier afternoon
- Many younger cows enter a second or even third breeding cycle after the initial breeding cycle if still not bred
- Bull elk are not looking to fight other bull elk unless they're closely invading their territory, bulls would much rather avoid conflict and take their cows elsewhere
- Elk lack an extensive sweat gland system that makes warmer temperatures very uncomfortable for them
- Elk prefer north and east facing slopes during the summer and warmer times as they provide cooler microclimates
- Elk prefer slopes less than 18 percent grade
- Elk prefer the upper third of a slope
- When you're calling, make sure they type of call will make sense for the time of year and other factors

- Try to create a "scenario" when you call so that it will appear more realistic to the elk

Chapter 5: Scouting

Scouting is without a doubt the most effective activity you can do to increase your success as a hunter. It's a relative equation, the more you put in, the more you'll get out. When most people think of scouting, they think about taking a trip out to the area they'll be hunting prior to the season, getting up early to observe the patterns of the animals or to roam the hillsides looking for trails with fresh sign. This type of scouting is definitely effective, but only part of the overall scouting equation. I consider there to be four types of scouting: data scouting, virtual scouting, telephone scouting, and physical scouting.

All four are effective and to some extent, necessary to increase your odds. Each one builds upon the other in beginning to identify and eliminate areas that will be of the least success as well as identifying areas where your odds will be higher. Let's take a look at each type of scouting individually and how they can be used to identify the highest percentage odds elk areas.

Data Scouting

You've probably never heard this term before but it can be an amazingly effective tool in finding high percentage elk areas to begin exploring further. Many Division of Wildlife offices publish statistics and information on their websites regarding previous year's harvest numbers, herd management plans, and big game unit hunting guides. I was astounded one time as I read through the notes of a herd management plan for deer and found an illustration showing the location of radio collared deer during winter in a certain region that I hunted. I almost busted out laughing as I looked at the area where I typically went (out of habit) and where the deer actually were. No wonder my success in that area had been lower than average, the deer were all on the other side of the mountain.

The real treasure though is the previous year's hunting statistics. These statistics can tell many stories when looked at with a critical eye. Data is available for each unit, season, species, and method of harvest that exist, along with numbers of hunters, number of days hunted, number of males harvested, number of females harvested, and percent success for each area and the season overall. Your particular state may be different in what they publish, but this is what I'm familiar with and is freely available on the Colorado Department of Wildlife (DOW) web site.

The DOW keeps more information than they publish; they also keep statistics on whether the hunter was resident or nonresident which gives interesting insight into the split of the success ratios. Areas with higher resident success and lower non-resident success can be indicative of units with a majority of the harvest coming from private land. I stumbled upon this data when I called the local DOW and requested the harvest data in non .pdf format. If you're handy with a computer and programs such as excel, having the raw data can be a very powerful tool in assessing areas based on a number of factors. If you can obtain copies of the data in some form of comma separated format (request a file called a .csv if they will provide it, Microsoft Excel can read these without any conversion), you can quickly begin to sort and filter data in such a way that will show you where the highest productivity areas are.

Here are a few key pieces of data to key in on:

Number of animals harvested – Obviously the higher the success ratio the better, however many areas will show up with very high success rates where only a few animals were taken. This may be due to a majority of private land, or perhaps the terrain is such that most hunters can't get back far enough to hunt. This is why it's important to look at the number of animals harvested overall instead of just the success ratio for the area. Remember, even if the area has quite a bit of hunting pressure, you can actually use that to your advantage. Most hunters won't go more than ½ mile from any road, and when we begin looking at virtual scouting techniques, I'll show you how to use hunting pressure to your advantage.

Number of bulls or number of cows – If you're a meat hunter, these numbers won't mean as much to you as the total number of animals harvested. I typically shoot the first legal animal to cross my path, with or without antlers. If you're primarily a trophy hunter, you'll want to find an area with a better than average bull harvest. If you can only get your hands on a cow tag due to preference points or some other limiting factor, then a high number of cows harvested will yield better chances of success.

Total recreational days – This metric is published in the Colorado harvest statistics so your state may vary; however it reveals quite an interesting bit of insight when looked at properly. If you take the total number of recreational days and divide it by the total number of animals harvested, you'll get an approximation of what I call "number of days hunted per animal." You may be looking at two areas that have near identical numbers of animals taken, however one may show 7 days per animal, and the other 21 days. This gives a rough estimation of how many days you should plan for in order to harvest an animal. 21 days may be way too long for you to hunt even if you may have a chance at a monster bull if you set up a spike camp deep in the wilderness.

In any case, try to choose an area where the effort required for success is in line with your available time.

Total number of hunters – As I said above, don't shy away too quickly from areas where a lot of people hunt. I've been crowded more times than I care to think about, but I also remember when I was crowded that I was hunting the easy spots right off main trails. Hunting pressure can actually be a good thing depending on whether or not the animals have easy access to private land (in which case they'll usually all be there after first season). Also whether or not you're willing to get up a little earlier than the rest of the crowd and take a position along a natural escape route.

Herd Statistics – Take a look at your local Department of Wildlife website, chances are that they publish statistics on the herds that exist in your hunting area. Statistics include valuable information such as the bull to cow ratio (important if you have your heart set on taking a bull) and overall herd numbers. Over time, if you collect this data or if the DOW site has multiple years, you can get an idea of whether or not the herd is in an up or down cycle. Several years ago my hunting partner and I found out the hard way that the harsh winters had taken their toll on the overall numbers in one of our "sure bet" areas. Had we known this, our plans would have most certainly been different.

Pay attention as well to any meetings the Department of Wildlife may hold in areas of interest, especially when they're soliciting input for their herd management plans. If you can attend, not only will you get some fantastic networking in with local landowners, but you'll also get valuable information regarding the herd you're interested in. By shear accident, I found out that quite a few local landowners attend these meetings to complain about the elk destroying their property! What an excellent opportunity to meet potential private property owners and gain permission to hunt their land.

The Internet

The internet has become my tool of choice for finding new areas to elk hunt and getting tidbits of information about areas that I'm interested in. First of all, hunters love to talk and tell stories. You wouldn't believe how many times I've come across incredibly valuable nuggets of information in chat forums and scattered in the most unlikely places. The reason most people don't actually find this information is that they don't know how to look for it. The internet is a sea of information and a general search will typically return something like 1.6 million results in .00456 seconds. The trick is thinking like a search engine and making sure the top 20 results you get back are the most valuable of those 1.6 million.

Everyone speaks a little differently, and many folks who are talking about the same thing will say it a different way. Take one of Colorado's game management units, unit 12. Unit 12 has some excellent public land hunting and it's no secret that quite a large number of elk are harvested in this unit every year. When you talk to someone about this unit though, they may refer to it as unit 12, GMU 12, game management unit #12, or the flat tops. I'm a big fan of Google, the results I get make sense to me and I know how to begin refining to get more of what I want. Here are a few tips to help you start getting more relevant results for your searches:

- Use the word "forum" in your searches. Like I said, hunters love to talk, but plenty of them love to type as well. There are hundreds of excellent websites out there for hunters and most of them will contain a decent question and answer forum. By simply adding the word "forum" to your search, you'll typically get back results where hunters are actually talking about the area you're interested in.

- Try different names – One never knows what another hunter may be calling an area. Searches for "flat tops elk Colorado" will return very different results than "unit 12 elk Colorado" or even "GMU 12 elk Colorado." Each one of these may lead to an excellent tip, starting point, or contact. I've been very surprised to find how helpful some folks will be on the internet in many forums. Don't be shy about asking for help, but also remember that chances are many hunters don't want to advertise everything in a public forum. If you come across someone who seems to have some good insight into an area you're interested in hunting, most sites (after you join for free) have a function to let you send the member a private message by clicking on their name and selecting that option. I've gotten turn by turn directions from some very nice and helpful people out there doing just this.

- Use quotes – Quotation marks can really help you separate the good from the irrelevant. If you type into the search engine something like the following:

Elk hunting unit 12 Colorado

You're bound to get back a few hundred results in the first few pages and many of them will have the number 12 in the time it was posted, or maybe someone drove 12 miles to their camp off highway 12. If you want to get greater relevancy in your results, the same query typed like the following will typically give you better odds:

Elk Hunting "Unit 12" Colorado

Pope and Young Records

Most of you are probably familiar with Pope and Young, the Pope and Young club has been around for decades and keeps the records of all exceptional bow hunting harvests for many big game species including elk. What most folks don't know is that Pope and Young also records all kinds of relevant statistical information about elk. Information such as age of hunter, years of hunting experience, time of day, hunting style, etc. is included.

For the most part, ordering the program and recording period statistical summary will give you the most recent information, including the state and county of harvest, the full big game records book is really just a large list of all the trophies to date with minimal information about the record. The real treat is the CD that comes with the full big game records book. This allows you to look at the data from several different facets with a little knowledge about simple applications such as Microsoft Excel. For example, the number one county for Pope and Young class bulls is Catron County in New Mexico with 490 records, coming in at a close second, Coconino County in Arizona has 479 records. Most of the other North American areas don't even come close to these two. There is some value in reviewing this information if you're going after a monster bull, however pure meat hunters may only find value in the statistics showing that the most effective methods for harvesting elk are spot and stalk and calling, and that the most consistent times of day are between 8AM and 10AM, and after 4PM.

Boone and Crockett

Where Pope and Young only records bow hunting statistics, Boone and Crockett records detailed information about animals taken via any manner of take. The most substantial difference though in the records is that the Boone and Crockett record books have much more detailed information about each recorded entry. Boone and Crockett now publishes a book with nothing but information on elk which is chock full of information including an individual recap of the hunt written by the hunter. Besides making for excellent and exciting reading, many of the stories contain valuable information regarding the details of the hunt, details that can be used to your advantage when hunting similar areas.

Virtual Scouting

We are so unbelievably blessed to live in a day and age where information is at our fingertips 24 hours a day. Before the advent of the Internet, it was difficult if not impossible to see an area without putting a few miles on your boot leather, and many out of state hunters didn't have the means to get to an area before their season and scout. Nowadays, I'm completely familiar with an area before I ever set foot in it and can recognize features I've seen on a computer monitor without ever having been there. There are a few programs that can are amazingly helpful in virtually scouting an area, and don't worry if you're not a computer genius, I'll walk you through it step by step.

Google Earth – Google earth allows you to scout an area using actual satellite photos that unveil amazing detail for having been taken from space. You may have seen areas while searching the internet on Google Maps, which are essentially the same pictures, just delivered to your browser (Internet Explorer or Firefox) instead of a program. There's a lot you can do with just the internet version of Google Maps, you can zoom in and out of an area, switch from aerial photos to colored maps that show some features like roads and larger landmarks, but to really get the full picture, you'll need something more powerful, that's Google Earth. Don't worry; Google Earth is a free download that will allow you to do all of the above plus a whole lot more.

Before we get into the nitty-gritty of how to scout using Google Earth, I wanted to cover something I've wished for countless times in other books but never found. As I spent my time reading book after book on elk hunting, they would all talk about the same types of terrain features. Words such as draws, fingers, funnels, points, ridgelines, valleys, saddles, benches and the like were thrown out there like I was supposed to know exactly what they meant and exactly how to identify these types of terrain both on a map an in the field. By the time we get done here, you'll be able to do just that. Below you'll find a list of each type of terrain feature we'll discuss along with a description of the geological features, what draws elk to them, and pictures of what they look like on both map and in real life.

Saddle

Description: A Saddle is a low spot between two mountains or hills, typically very close together. From the side, they look like a saddle you'd put on a horse, hence the name.

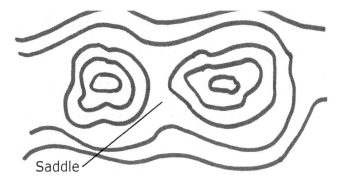

Saddle

What draws elk to them: Saddles are natural crossing points for elk to cross between areas when they want to move. Elk will always take the path of least resistance and a saddle offers a lower elevation spot to cross thereby expending less energy (something we know elk are very interested in). Hunters can use saddles as ambush points to catch elk as they pass through this area.

Fingers or Finger Ridges

Description: Some people call them finger ridges, others just refer to them as fingers, but these areas actually look like a giant's hand was laid flat on the ground and you were looking up from the tip of the giant's finger to the top of his hand. There are typically many of them in a row and the sides are usually steep on their way up to a flat area. Most of these fingers have drainages between them.

What draws elk to them: Finger ridges that face east tend to have more forage for elk than other areas due to the greater moisture, less sun exposure, and protection from harsh winds. Elk can feed in a somewhat isolated and protected environment in these areas.

Hill

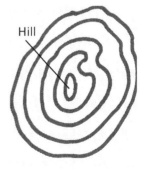

Description: Simply put, a hill is normally a bell shaped mass of land that rises and falls in all directions. You'll know if you're on a hill when you're at the top and you're surrounded by downhill on all sides.

What draws elk to them: Hills or mountains offer highly elevated ground. This can be important to elk certain times of the year such as summer when elk seek these higher elevations looking for cooler weather. Elk may also seek relief from biting flies and insects in these upper regions as winds are typically stronger.

Ridge

Description: A ridge is similar to a bunch of hills that are touching each other before they descend all the way back down to their original elevation. If you're having trouble picturing this, simply make a fist and look at your knuckles. This forms a natural ridge as the height of your knuckles will remain higher across your hand than any low point where the "ridge" falls off toward your palm. Contour lines that form a ridge tend to be in the shape of a U or the shape of a V, whereas contour lines for a hill are typically shaped like an O.

What draws elk to them: Ridges are just a natural formation in most heavily wooded areas. Elk will typically haunt areas where they're undisturbed, where they can watch for danger, and where

there's cover to escape to. Most areas you find elk will just naturally have ridges given what we know about elk especially that
they prefer sloping ground and the top third of

Bench

Description: A bench is a spot where the land flattens out temporarily on its way down the mountain. Benches can be either long
and run all the way alongside the sloped area, or can be small little
"pocket" benches where the land just flattens out for a few hundred
yards in width and then resumes its natural slope downward.

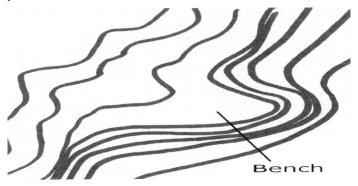

What draws elk to them: Elk love benches for several reasons.
Elk can cross mountainous terrain much more easily on a flattened
bench and will do so versus walking on the more uneven hillside.
Elk also like to bed down on benches as it allows them to stay
where they like to be (on the side of a mountain) on a flat surface
with an excellent view of any danger that may be coming from
below.

103

Valley

Description: A valley is simply level ground with higher ground on either side of it. If you find a stream on a map, chances are it has cut a valley through the terrain over time. This doesn't mean that there has to be a stream near the bottom, a valley can just be a normally occurring geographic feature.

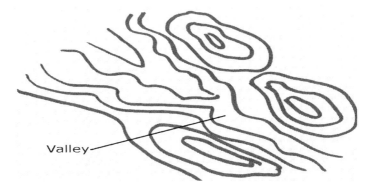

What draws elk to them: Valleys offer protection to elk as they move from area to area. Visibility into valleys is typically restricted to being on one of the two hillsides which makes for excellent sneaking grounds for elk.

Gulch

Description: A steep walled valley, usually cut by a stream running through it. Refer to valley above for information.

Draw

Description: A draw is very much like a valley except they typically don't have long runs like a valley does and are typically located on the side of a ridge. A draw typically looks like someone took a pie wedge shaped slice out of the side of a hill or mountain. A draw is very similar to a valley but less developed.

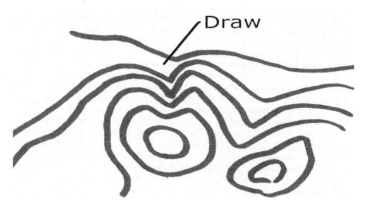

What draws elk to them: Draws are typically cut into the mountainside by floods or higher pressure waters cutting through the dirt on their way down. Draws offer a secluded spot for elk to traverse a hill as the terrain is lower than the sides keeping them out of sight. Draws typically lure me in for scaling a mountain as the water can many times clear brush out of the way leaving stair-like rocks for me to climb; perhaps the elk are no different?

Scouting Paper Maps

Paper maps are typically where I start my scouting from on a new area once I've done my data scouting. To me, the most valuable for the first step of scouting are the BLM Maps as they show a good topographic overview and also land ownership. BLM maps are available for most all states where you can hunt elk, they run about $4 each and can be ordered either online at http://publiclands.org/home.php or by calling your local BLM field office. The advantage of paper maps is that you can easily draw on them which will be a key attribute for narrowing down areas to investigate. Hopefully data scouting has yielded some decent results and you have some ideas of where the elk are. You may or may not find exact locations to hunt, however if you even find fellow hunters naming areas, within your unit of interest, it's much better than starting from scratch. Once you have your paper map, get at least two different colored highlighters (I suggest one green and one yellow), a black pen, a red permanent marker and get ready for some fun.

Step by step map investigation

1. Outline your GMU unit boundaries – This can be a little tough, but it's pretty logical. Most game management unit boundaries follow major roads or logical features. The Department of wildlife for your area of interest will most likely publish a map of the GMU's as well as the description of where the boundaries lie. Take your yellow marker and draw in the borders of the GMU you're interested in.

2. Pinpoint areas you know about – These inputs can be from data scouting, tips from friends or relatives, or areas mentioned by your phone scouting efforts. Circle these areas on your map with the black pen, write what it is of interest about

it (draw, bench, etc.) and then highlight it in yellow.

3. Eliminate low percentage areas – This is where red permanent marker comes in. Look at your map scale, on BLM maps, each 1 inch box equals 1 mile. Some boxes are easy and obvious to eliminate such as areas with no cover, populated areas, areas consisting of only private land (which you can find by utilizing BLM maps), and areas with excessive roads or highways going through them. These areas may hold elk, but our goal is to eliminate greater than 90% of the area on the map so we can focus on productive areas. If a box has the attributes listed above, simply outline the box in red and move on to the next.

4. Eliminate impossible areas – Wherever you're going, you have to be able to get there. Areas that are extremely difficult as shown by elevation lines that are very close together or greater than say three miles from any forest roads or trails are probably going to be unreachable by mere mortals. If an area seems particularly interesting though, don't discount taking a peek on Google Earth as we'll learn about later or calling the local forest service office to see if any logging roads might exist. Also, know your limits. If you're out of shape and know you won't be able to climb to the top of an 11,000 foot mountain, eliminate those areas, it's better to show up with a realistic plan than to have to throw out your plan when you arrive before hunting season. Outline these boxes in red and move on to the next box.

5. Find areas to investigate. We'll take this further later on when

we view these areas on the computer and call local Game Wardens and Wildlife Biologists, but here's a little tip. If you see a large mass of land and a few landmarks, maybe some places with names with gulch or draw in them (lost gulch, forkhorn draw, etc), take note of these areas for further investigation. They're easier to find on maps, you may find tidbits of information about them by typing them into Google Search Engine, and wildlife professionals typically know them by name so you'll be speaking a common language. Try to find forested areas with terrain features that such as water, saddles, benches, valleys and the like. The more of these types of areas, the better the chances elk will hold up in them. Circle any of these areas with the yellow highlighter.

6. Look for access into areas – On BLM maps, trails are shown with dashed lines. Areas where trails reach deep back into the timber will be more readily accessible to hunters on foot. Now keep in mind that these areas will draw other hunters too, however most hunters won't venture more than a mile or so down a trail. You can actually use this to your advantage as we identify escape routes that other hunters will push elk to.

7. Identify areas with high probability features – as you analyze each box looking for clues such as north or east facing slopes for early season hunting, south facing slopes for winter hunting, benches, saddles, appropriate elevations, etc., make small notes on your map. If an area holds one or more high probability features, take out your green highlighter and outline that area. This will be an area for further investigation.

After completing this exercise your map should be well marked up. Examine the areas shown in green further with the steps outlined in the next sections.

Scouting Virtual Maps

Now that we've covered some of the more common types of terrain and what they look like, let me key you in on a way to find these areas without ever leaving the comfort of your computer. Virtual scouting is one of the most effective scouting methods I've ever used and the information is freely available. There are several tools to do this with that are free such as ArcGIS Explorer, however I've been using Google Earth for quite a while now so that's my tool of choice. There's an excellent DVD out that GMUResearch.com put together that walks you through these steps using ArcGIS Explorer if you just can't pick things up without seeing them.

The first step is to download Google Earth. Google Earth is a GIS (Geographic Information System) tool that uses terraservers (Computers containing information and pictures about the earth) to allow the user to view areas of the world at different scales. As you zoom in on an area, Google Earth will actually begin pulling in maps with more and more definition all the way down to USGS 7.5 topographic maps (once added). It's important to understand that Google Earth works by applying layers. Imagine for a second you took some transparent sheets of plastic and several colored markers. If you drew a mountain on one sheet and then laid it down on the counter, then drew scattered trees on the same spot on another sheet then laid that down on top of the first, then finally drew some streams on a third sheet and laid it down over the first two, you'd have a picture that looked like terrain and wouldn't really be able to tell it was on three separate sheets.

Google Earth works much the same way in that you can take a picture that has a topographic map, then on top of that place an aerial or satellite photo of the area, then over that place shaded shapes representing GMU's or areas of elk use (something we'll actually do shortly). You can even set the transparency of each layer so that you can see through and view multiple layers at once. Doing this allows you want to look at an actual aerial photo of your perspective hunting grounds, but also "lightly" display the topographic map features of it as well so that you can identify both topographic and aerial images.

Google Earth is free for home use and since the first edition of this book, Google has changed their licensing model and made their pro version free as well. The pro version used to cost $400 per license and there are some amazing things you can do with it now such as see parcel ownership overlays and import/convert other shape file types. One other thing to understand about Google Earth is that it's pulling in information as you move and zoom. It doesn't actually download all of the earth's images to your computer; it pulls in only the areas you look at as you look at them. Keep this in mind as sometimes it takes a second for Google Earth to pull the information and display it to you, but it's well worth the wait. So let's get started.

Installing Google Earth

The first thing you'll need to do is to actually download and install Google Earth. Open your web browser, type in the address below and click the appropriate installation for your system (usually windows).

http://earth.google.com

Click through all the install steps and just take the default settings for each screen until you reach the finish screen (you may wish to deselect the checkbox that tries to install Google Chrome). Once you're finished, we're ready to have some fun.

Finding areas in Google Earth

The first task we'll look at is actually finding your area of interest. There are several boxes to your left; the first box is the search box as shown in this section.

If you know exactly where your area is, you can simply begin to zoom in closer and closer until you find it (you start from a view of the earth from outer space), but locating a nearby town or land-

mark is much easier. You can type the actual name of the location you're looking for, if Google Earth doesn't find it, try searching for a nearby city, town, or mountain, and then you can find it from there. There are three tabs in the search box, you'll use the default "fly to" tag. When the area or town shows up within the search box below, simply click it and Google Earth will zoom in to the location you requested.

Moving around in Google Earth

Moving around in Google Earth is fairly simple. If your mouse has a wheel on it, you'll notice by rolling the mouse wheel back and forth that Google Earth will zoom in and out to different levels of detail. Moving North, South, East and West is accomplished by clicking and holding the left button on your mouse and then "dragging" the direction you want them map to move. Once you see the section you're interested in, simply let go of the mouse button and Google Earth will stop right there. If your mouse doesn't have a scroll wheel on it, or if you're more comfortable with the keyboard, here are a few keyboard shortcuts that do the same thing.

- Up/Down/Right/Left arrow keys: Moves the view in the direction of the arrow, North, South, East, West respectively
- + key: Zoom in
- - key: Zoom out

Play around a little bit until you get comfortable with viewing the aerial images, next we'll look at getting a little more advanced.

Adding topographic maps to Google Earth

Topographic maps require you to link to a USGS server. Remember, you'll be adding an additional layer so things may change suddenly (such as if you had put a non-transparent sheet in your picture stack). Follow the steps below to add the topographic maps to Google Earth.

For your convenience, I've located all the links listed in this book at the following address:

http://www.coloradohunters.net

1. Create a new folder on your computer's hard drive under the c:\ drive called huntingGIS (we'll use this folder extensively)

2. Download the .kmz file by typing the following address into your internet browser:

http://www.earthpoint.us/TopoMap.aspx

3. When it asks you what to do with the file, save the file to the folder you just created at c:\huntingGIS

4. Switch to Google Earth application

5. Click Open at the top left of the Google Earth Toolbar

6. Navigate to the c:\huntingGIS folder and select the topo-maps.kmz file

7. Notice that in the layers box on the left side, you now see a layer named USGS topo maps, you should also see topographic maps changing to greater levels of detail as you zoom in on areas by rolling the wheel on your mouse back and forth.

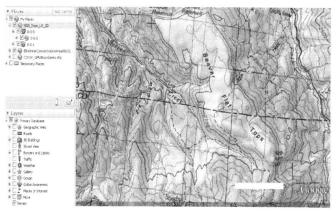

Image USDA Farm Service Agency ©2010 Google

Remember that Google Earth continually pulls information from the server each time you change what you view, so depending on your internet connection speed, this may take a few seconds. If the map continually refreshes, right click on the layer named USGS topo maps and click "properties". The last tab named refresh will allow you to set the refresh to on demand instead of automatic by changing the "View Based Refresh" drop down to "On Request"

Setting the Transparency of a Layer

Remember earlier when we thought about layers as clear sheets of plastic that we could draw on? Only if the sheets were clear could we see the ones beneath the top sheet. Layers in

114

Google Earth can also be set to be more transparent, or more opaque, allowing you to see multiple layers at the same time. Follow the steps below to set the transparency of the topographic layer:

1. Click on the layer you wish to adjust the transparency of, in this case, click the topo layer you just added so that it is highlighted in blue

2. Click the slider bar underneath the layer list labeled "transparency"

3. Move the slider bar to the left and right to see how the layer gets more or less transparent. Find a level that you can still see the topographic lines, yet can also see the actual aerial photographs underneath.

Hopefully you can begin to see how powerful this feature is. Now you can view the topographic features we've identified above, while still retaining the ability to view actual terrain features such as unmarked trails, logging roads, and cover types such as pine and aspen.

As you can see in the image above, all of my imported layers are under "My Places". By default, Google Earth will bring them into the location where you have focus when you're importing the

115

layer. It's easy to move layers though, you can just drag and drop them to a folder of your choosing. The "Temporary Places" folder is cleared each time you shut down Google Earth so if you want to keep your files handy, move them up to a more permanent location.

Changing your viewing direction

This is a very handy tip as Google Earth defaults to showing terrain with a North oriented map. You may want to view the terrain from the direction you'd enter it along a trail, or perhaps you'd like to view it from the perspective of looking east to identify south facing slopes if the time of year dictates. You can easily change the orientation of the map by executing the following steps:

- On the toolbar at the top of the screen click the view menu, select the "Show Navigation" section, and select automatic, To the right, you'll notice a small circle with N S E W at the appropriate points of the circle with a small triangle pointing to the N as shown in the accompanying illustration

©2010 Google

- Position your mouse over the triangle, hold down the left button on your mouse, and drag the triangle around the circle to change the orientation

Changing View Perspective

Pretty cool so far huh? But wait! There's more, and I've actually saved the best for last. Can you imagine having a birds-eye view of your hunting area from any angle?

Having the ability to actually see how the terrain flows, where the natural valleys, escape routes, saddles and benches are? Well with Google Earth, you can do just that.

You have the ability to see any location from any position (looking North, South, East, or West) and most any elevation from level with the ground to hovering 1000 feet above. Here's how to do it:

1. Zoom in close to the area you're interested in, close enough so that you can view a few square miles of area

2. Place your mouse pointer in the center of the screen

3. Press and hold the shift key on your keyboard (don't let it up)

4. Now press and hold the left mouse button so the pointer turns into a fist icon

5. Move the mouse downward dragging the view closer to the bottom of the screen

Image USDA Farm Service Agency ©2010 Google

You should now see the view of the terrain as you would if you were hovering in a helicopter hundreds of feet above the mountain. You can do this at any level of zoom and it's amazingly effective in truly understanding what the physical terrain looks like. Do you see valleys, saddles, and mountains? Using this technique you should be able to identify natural corridors that elk will use to escape hunting pressure and to migrate from one area to another using the route of least effort. Remember too that you can perform all of the steps above through any view. You can change the orientation while the perspective is tilted so you can virtually "fly" around an area to see all angles, or spin your view around from the top of a mountain to see what terrain would look like in any direction (especially helpful for identifying those pesky north facing slopes).

Importing and Exporting GPS Waypoints and Routes to your Map

©2010 Google

One of the most amazing things you can do with Google Earth and other GIS browser type software is to create waypoints directly on the map and then export them into your GPS or vice versa. It's incredibly handy to be able to mark exact locations when identifying escape routes and natural corridors, and then put them right into your GPS so there's no question once you get there that you are in the correct spot.

I've found this feature also useful for navigating thin strips of public land that wind through private areas. Many of these areas exist where a square mile or two is surrounded by private land and offers only a small strip of public access. These areas can pay big dividends as many hunters either won't know how to get to them, or won't feel comfortable that their access route doesn't include trespassing.

In the GPS world, waypoints are markers that you'll usually create while out in the field so you can find your way back to a particular spot. In this case, we'll be creating them from the computer without ever being there. To create a waypoint, find the point you'd like to place the waypoint on the map, right click, and select "Save to My Places." You should see your newly created waypoint in the "Places" box on the left of the screen.

The next section will cover creating routes, but the import and export of them follow the same steps.

To Import your existing waypoints/routes from your GPS, simply perform the following steps

1. Click on Tools, then select GPS
2. Select your Model of GPS from the two choices (Magellan or Garmin)
3. Plug in your GPS

4. Click Import

      Your existing GPS data will be pulled into your Google Earth session for your viewing pleasure. There are unfortunately far too many GPS units out there to include detailed steps for importing these files, so I've only covered the two most common brands that have a built in import to Google Earth. If you happen to own a different brand, type the brand of the GPS into Google Search along with the words "import waypoint file" without the quotes. You should find a tutorial for how to do it considering that most GPS units these days offer this functionality.

      Exporting waypoints and routes is a bit more complicated and there is no built in functionality. I prefer a free utility called GPS Utility that makes the process fairly easy. Once you've downloaded and installed the utility from http://www.gpsu.co.uk, you can begin importing route files that have been exported from Google Earth. To export routes or waypoints, follow the steps below:

1. Right click on the route or waypoint
2. Select "Save Place As"
3. Make sure that the file type in the bottom drop down says .kml, not .kmz
4. Save the file to a location you'll be able to find it during the next step (such as your desktop, or my documents)

To import the .kml file to your GPS

1. Plug your GPS into the computer (you may need to reference your owner's manual for instructions)

2. Open GPS Utility

3. If this is the first time you've connected, select GPS from the menu on top, then click setup. There is a built in help section to assist you in configuring your GPS. If you've already performed this step, click "connect"

4. Select File from the top menu, then select Open

5. Find the .kml file that you wish to import and select it

6. Select GPS from the top menu, then select Upload all

Creating a Route in Google Earth

Routes are simply a series of waypoints connected to give you a path (not necessarily a straight line) to where you want to get to. Creating a route is easy, but not as intuitive as one would hope. To create a route, try the following steps:

1. Ensure that the complete area you want the route to go through is visible on the screen

2. Click on Add on the toolbar at the top of the screen, then choose Path

3. A dialog box should pop up for the new Path, this is where things are not very intuitive as you must move the dialog box off to the side so you can see the map, do this by left clicking and holding on the top part of the window where it says "New Path", then drag the window off to the side and out of the way

4. Left click once where you want your route to start, and then simply click to draw straight, connected lines to where you want to go.

5. Double click on the spot which should be the end of your path

6. Click on the dialog box that you moved to the side, give the route a name and then click OK

The final route should look something like the image to the right. You can adjust the color and line thickness by right clicking on the name of the route in the layers list and selecting properties.

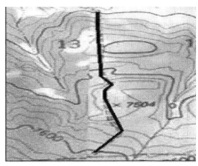

Image USDA Farm Service Agency
©2010 Google

For those of you hunting in Colorado, I'm going to include some steps that are absolutely amazing for hunting here in my home state. I'll list a few other resources I've found too towards the end of this chapter, but if your state isn't listed, you may want to do some poking around on the internet or call your local Division of Wildlife to see if similar resources exist.

Converting Between GIS Formats

This is where things may get a little too technical and very confusing, so I've taken the liberty of converting the freely available shapefiles and converted them into Google Earth native formats. The process itself isn't terribly complex; just note that like with anything, there are various companies competing to make their format the standard. Google Earth uses .kml or .kmz files and other programs such as ArcGIS Explorer use .shp files. As I mentioned earlier, Google Earth Pro is now free for home use and has

122

the ability to convert .shp files to .kml/kmz files and immediately import them into Google Earth. Simply click on File>Import, find the file you'd like to convert, and click "Open". If you don't see the file you're looking for, check the drop down box next to the file name box and either change it to all files or the file type you're trying to convert.

Overlaying Game Management Units (GMUs) on your map

If you're lucky enough to live in a state that publishes overlays of the game management boundaries, you can easily download the overlay and see exactly which unit you're looking at. Since I live in Colorado, I'll use the Colorado GMU overlay as an example, but don't fear, the link below offers a list of GMU overlays for most states that offer them:

https://www.huntinfool.com/maps/googlemaps.php

Your browser will typically ask you if you want to open or save the file once you click a link, choose save. Save this file the c:\huntingGIS folder as you did with the topographic layer above, and then follow the steps below:

1. Run the conversion process to create the .kml file (skip this if you've downloaded them in .kml format already)
2. Click the file menu on the top toolbar and select open

3. Find the overlay file that you saved in the c:\huntingGIS\GMUs folder and select it

4. Click the Open button

5. The GMU's will open up in an outline mode which is the same as most other shapes, I prefer to randomize the colors

6. Right click on the boundaries entry in places and select properties

7. Click the Style/Color tab

8. Select "Share Style"

9. Click the "Random" checkbox, ensure that the "Color" Dropdown for Area says "filled", and set the opacity to 30% as shown.

10. Click Finish

Once completed, zoom out and you'll see each GMU in Colorado shaded in different colors.

Remember that you can turn any layer off, which does not permanently remove it, by simply unchecking the box next to it in the layers list.

Image USDA Farm Service Agency
Image © 2010 Digital Globe ©2010 Google

After adding the GMU's, don't forget to adjust the transparency of the view so you get the full benefit of the borders while still being able to see the underlying terrain features. You can easily turn this layer on and off by locating the GMU overlay in the layers are and deselecting it. Pay careful attention to step 11 in the list above as this information is useful with any layer. You can make them fully shaded as the picture above, or change the dropdown to "outline only" and simply see outlined views.

One other interesting feature when the GMU's are turned on is that sometimes you can get information about the individual GMU by simply clicking on it, The following image shows some of the information that is available to you for each GMU in Colorado.

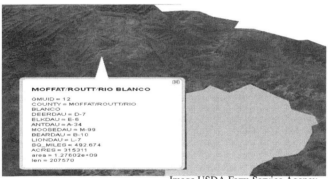

Image USDA Farm Service Agency
Image © 2010 Digital Globe ©2010 Google

Adding Game Animal Activity layers

If you weren't having enough fun just looking at satellite photos with topographic overlays and GMU shading, next we'll have some real fun by adding layers for actual game animal activities right onto your map view. The Natural Diversity Information System (NDIS) is a site that collects information regarding elk overall range, summer and winter concentration areas, migration corridors, etc. for Colorado. They used to offer all of this information free of charge in a format that Google Earth can import right onto your map, however it appears they've discontinued it and put all the information online in their own tool that we'll cover later. Luckily I pulled the files down for Colorado and saved them to the site below. For other states, try a quick Google search.

http://www.coloradohunters.net

Image USDA Farm Service Agency
Image © 2010 Digital Globe ©2010 Google

These files can be downloaded, saved into your c:\huntingGIS directory and opened in Google Earth just like the GMU and topographic layers. This is amazingly useful information. With these layers, you'll be able to see exactly where the elk tend to concentrate during any season. Combine that with your ability to view topographic features, tilt to get a bird's eye view of the terrain, and see where trails exist and different types of cover meet, and you've got a powerful tool. Use this resource to isolate where your best odds for success would be before you ever set foot in the field.

Adding Land Ownership Information

In addition to adding the game activity areas, there are also layers available that show various aspects of land ownership. This can be incredibly handy for determining national forest and wildlife area boundaries, as well as private land ownership.

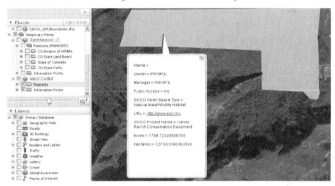

Image USDA Farm Service Agency
Image © 2010 Digital Globe ©2010 Google

Keep in mind though that many of these resources may be out of date so make sure you verify that you're not trespassing. The Colorado Hunting Atlas, which we'll look at shortly, has a handy checkbox called "land manager" in the layer list. When you turn this on, it shows what appears to be all the state and federal land information such as state lands, national forest, etc. This is one of my favorite layers to toggle on and off using the checkbox in the layer list. It makes it easy to ensure that the area you're looking at is truly public land. BLM maps or their equivalent are helpful as well, just remember, the responsibility is on the hunter to ensure that we know the boundaries of public and private land. If you live in Colorado, you can download the BLM and National Forest lands from ***http://www.coloradohunters.net***. . For other states, you may have to do a quick Google Search for "national forest overlay google earth". The following location had a comprehensive list of states:

http://apeoid.com/kmz-kml-padus/

For Those Not to "comfortable" with Computer "Voodoo": Web Hunting Maps

If you're not too comfortable with all the steps we've discussed to install Google Earth and manipulate it, don't worry. There's a simple way to get most of the information listed above if your hunt will take place in Colorado. Colorado Parks and wildlife offers a site called the Colorado Hunting Atlas where they essentially expose to you all of the layers I mentioned above and then some. You'll lose the ability to tilt and move very quickly through terrain as each time the screen changes, it has to do a full refresh, but if you have an older computer that just can't handle Google Earth, this will give you many of the capabilities that I mentioned before, but using only your web browser. To access this information, type the following link into the address bar of your web browser:

http://ndismaps.nrel.colostate.edu/index.html?app=HuntingAtlas

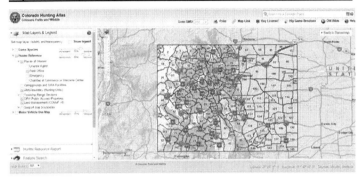

©Natural Diversity Information Source

You'll see immediately in the top middle of the screen you have the ability to jump straight to your GMU of choice. The easiest way to find specific places is similar to finding them in Google Earth. To the right, you'll see a small search box, simply type your area in there and a small pop up window will appear showing possible results for your search. Click on the one that's correct and mapit will take you to that area. To the left, you'll also see multiple check boxes for different layers you can add on such as land ownership, national forest, etc. Up near the top, you'll find a link that says "Game Species", by clicking it, you'll see many new layers that you can add to your list of layer selections including elk overall range, winter and summer concentrations, migration routes, etc. Select as many as you're interested in and they will appear in the main layer list allowing you to then add them to your map.

Other Virtual Scouting Resources

Game Maps for Montana:
Download shapefiles from
http://fwp.mt.gov/doingBusiness/reference/gisData

Hunting information for Idaho
Tons of great information in both .shp and native Google Earth .kml files
http://fishandgame.idaho.gov/ifwis/huntplanner/download.aspx

GPS Utility:
A free tool for importing and exporting routes and waypoints to your GPS
http://www.gpsu.co.uk

Telephone Scouting

Telephone scouting is an important tool, I wouldn't take the next step of physical scouting until you've thoroughly performed this step and have adequate information. The two steps performed prior to this one are key in preparation for this step as you must have some insight into where you'd like to hunt prior to getting on the phone. There are many resources out there that will be helpful in preparation for physical scouting trips and your actual hunt. Many hunters only think to call the most logical of resources such as the Game Warden for their area and the local Wildlife Biologist. We'll cover speaking to them shortly, but I wanted to provide you with some resources that you may not have thought about calling.

Game processing units and Taxidermy shops spend their hunting seasons watching elk come in their doors along with the proud hunter that harvested them. Hunters love to talk and chances are these Taxidermists and Processors know a thing or two about what areas their work is coming from. If you're going to take advantage of their services, so much the better! Let them know that you're a potential customer and ask them some intelligent questions about the surrounding areas. These resources are much more likely to answer a question like "Where are all the good elk spots?" versus a wildlife professional, but be prepared to have some intelligent conversations with them to involving specific areas that you've identified. Chances are they live locally and know the mountain/valley/gulch that you're speaking of and can give you some good insight into it. Once again, local folks know the area and are usually in tune with what's going on. Don't discount the knowledge of local haunts such as fly-fishing shops where they may provide guide services and spend a good amount of time in the same types of areas you're interested in hunting. Smaller sporting goods stores that are selling gear and ammunition to their yearly crowd can also be good resources.

Speaking to Wildlife Professionals

I want you to imagine for a second that you got your dream job as a Game Warden or Wildlife Biologist. You spend quite a bit of time in the field, seeing animals, counting herds, talking to good natured hunters in the forest, sounds great doesn't it? Now imagine that job the week before big game season opens in that area. Your phone is ringing off the hook. Not only do you have your normal job to do, but now you've got to answer and return calls from hundreds of hunters. You're swamped! It doesn't seem like you're ever going to get caught up. All of a sudden the phone in front of you rings again, you pick it up, and there's a hunter from another area calling and says, "So I was thinking of hunting GMU 12, can you tell me where to go to get an elk?." I can almost guarantee the answer, it will go something like this, "Well, there are elk all over unit 12, almost anywhere you go will have elk in it." If you hunt Colorado and know unit 12, take a peek at what you're now up against. This is a big unit with thousands of acres of forest. That kind of answer isn't nearly specific enough to be helpful and setting out without a clear plan is a recipe for tag soup.

Wildlife professionals actually work for the public. Your tax dollars pay their salary and part of their job is to take your calls and answer your questions. These good folks are not there to hinder your success either. They set game quotas as a way to control the herd for the local area and they count on a certain percentage of hunters being successful to help them meet their objectives. They can be very helpful and a wealth of information, but they respect hunters who do their homework. I can guarantee you too that if you find one who will answer the "Where do I hunt" question, he or she is telling everyone else that exact same tidbit of information and you'll be up to your neck in competition.

The better prepared you are to talk to these folks, the better the quality of information you're going to get. If you've spent your time doing your data and virtual scouting, you'll be well prepared to have an intelligent conversation with these folks. They'll recognize your preparation and reward you with useful information instead of the canned answers they give to less prepared hunters.

One last tip before we get into exactly what questions to ask and what to do with that information, try to avoid yes or no questions. They're too easy and won't spur conversations that might lead to information you hadn't even thought of asking. When you write down your list of questions prior to your call, read them over and make sure there are no yes/no type questions, if there are, try to reword them like the example that follows:

Yes/No type question: "I was thinking of hunting bighorn draw on opening morning, are there a lot of elk in there?"

Open ended question: "I noticed that there was a funnel in bighorn draw, how would you hunt that area if you were going to be there on opening morning?"

Questions to ask Wildlife Professionals

Wildlife professionals are in fact public workers and part of their job is to respond to questions by the public. That does not mean though that they have hours to spend talking to you on the phone, so don't count on calling them blindly and having a great conversation about an area, even if you have done your research. Always have your list of questions prepared ahead of time and on a sheet of paper with plenty of room underneath each question to write down the response you are given. I've had to move to a second or third sheet many times when you hit the right person as they can give you so much information you can't fit it all on a single page.

There are some basic questions you should always ask when researching a new area, plus you should have quite a few questions just from pouring over the maps and scouting. I'll get you started on some of the more general questions that you might wish to ask.

Game Wardens

Question: What is the overall condition of the elk herd in that area?

Relevance: Elk are subject to many factors including predators, snowfall, and human pressures such as logging or other forestry activities. You'll want to know if something significant has happened lately.

134

Question: How do the elk use this area? Do they stay year round or migrate through?

Relevance: The answer to this may determine the time of year this area will best produce.

Question: How much hunting pressure does this area get? Where do the hunters typically access from and how many hunters should I expect to see in a day if I get more than a mile off the main roads/trails?

Relevance: You'll want to know how much company you'll have and what they're likely to be doing. Elk will move out as hunters move in and if you can identify the escape routes, you can use the hunting pressure to your advantage.

Question: What's the best way to access the area I'm interested in? What kinds of terrain is it, can I walk freely or is it very thick with brush? Are there trails or logging roads that aren't on the map?

Relevance: If the area is only accessible via migrating through dark timber or through some steep and dangerous areas, you may wish to pass. Remember, you also have to get your elk out of there too!

Question: Are there areas that have open views for glassing if I wanted to watch this area for game activity? Where are they and EXACTLY how would I get there?

Relevance: Glassing is one of the most effective methods for mapping big game. It's very difficult to identify whether or not that excellent looking location on the map is covered with trees to the point where it obscures your view. Ask how to get there and ask them to give you as much detail as possible. A helpful tip is to ask if they have a BLM map handy, when they're referring to a location, you can identify and confirm the exact grid position that it's on.

Question: How will the elk respond to hunting pressure? Where will they go when hunters begin entering the area? Do they tend to come back, if so, when?

Relevance: If you know where they're going, obviously you'll want to identify terrain features such as saddles and valleys they'll use to get there. I've had Wildlife professionals tell me the exact spot on private property they all go to once the pressure turns up. Also, if you're hunting in a second or third rifle season, you'll want to know what the earlier season pressure will do to the animals. If they head for private land and don't come back, you may need to think about a different season or hope for some weather to push them.

Question: Are there ATV trails in this area?

Relevance: You may want to think twice about hunting in areas with ATV's. ATV riders will be making all kinds of noise on opening day and elk aren't stupid, they'll move out very quickly.

Question: How much of this area is public land, how much is private? Will most of the animals in the area move to the private lands, if not, how much pressure will it take to push them there?

Relevance: Too much private land next to your hunting area can be a very bad situation. If the area gets a lot of pressure, and the elk know that safety is just a fence line away, they'll be gone before you know it.

Question: Are there outfitters that work this area or ranches near-by?

Relevance: This can be a good thing if they say yes. Outfitters typically don't waste their time in non-productive areas and private ranch hunting makes that private land less safe for the elk.

Question: What's the percentage of residents to non-residents that frequent this area? What are the success rates of each group?

Relevance: If you find areas where it's almost all residents, ask if it's because the public land hunting opportunities are limited or if it's mostly private land.

Question: What do the elk tend to feed on in this area? What elevation does that food tend to grow at? Are there areas of concentration?

Relevance: Find the food and you'll likely find the elk.

Question: What would it take to move the elk out of this area?

Relevance: You'll want to be prepared for any conditions that come along. If the Game warden tells you they'll move to lower ground if it snows, be ready with a lower ground backup plan in case of a snowstorm.

Question: What elevation holds the greatest concentration of elk? Specifically what do you consider to be high elevation, and what do you consider to be low elevation?

Relevance: Knowing which elevations will increase your odds will make identifying higher odds areas easier. Make sure that they're idea of low and high elevations are the same as yours!

Question: What would be the most effective method to hunt this area? Stand hunting? Spot and stalk? Still Hunting?

Relevance: Hopefully the Game Warden will clue you in on some great information here. Don't forget to ask them why they feel a certain method would be better. The more you understand about the area, the elk, and their behavior, the better.

Question: Have there been any burns in the area in the last few years? If so, where?

Relevance: Elk love to frequent burn areas that are in a re-growth period. The food is usually abundant and highly nutritious.

Question: If you were hunting this area, where would you go and how would you hunt it?

Relevance: Take this one with a grain of salt. They may tell you that tidbit they tell everyone else, but if they see you're serious, they may part with some valuable information.

Wildlife Biologists

Many of the same questions as above can be answered by Wildlife Biologists, and some even better. In my experience, Wildlife Biologists are more concerned with the elk's overall well-being, herd numbers, and behavior. They're well suited to answer questions that pertain to these areas, but they have in the past referred me to the local Game Warden for more detailed hunting questions.

Forest Service Officers

If you plan on hunting national forest, chances are there's a local Forest Service office that is responsible for that area. These officers spend quite a bit of time in the field and can answer many of the same questions listed in the Game Warden area.

Asking Specific Questions

Regardless of who you speak to, make sure you are prepared to hold an intelligent conversation and ask very specific, open-ended questions. If your virtual scouting techniques have yielded a nice looking saddle between public and private land, ask a question such as "I noticed there was a small saddle between bighorn gulch and deadfoot mountain, how will the elk use that as pressure builds in the hunting area? Have you seen other hunters using that area?" Have several plans of attack together and ask them which they think would be best and why.

I once got some great information from a Division of Wildlife Game Warden after calling and speaking with her several times. Our initial conversations revolved around a very specific area for which she gave me some great historical information. After about our third conversation and two physical scouting trips to the area, I asked her, "I noticed a fence line running down the top of the mountain leading away from the main trail, do you think my odds would be better hunting the escape route down the fence line versus the stock pond that we've been talking about?", I got a very enthusiastic "oh yes" to that question.

She wasn't willing to give up that information until I found it myself, but once asked, she was more than willing to tell me why that would be a better option. I ended up calling in four small groups of elk on opening morning in that exact spot, and a six point bull the next morning. The point is to do your homework first and well, and then ask them their opinion. I've had much better success sparking up valuable conversations when asking their assessment of my hunting plans versus asking them exactly where to go.

Physical Scouting

If you're lucky, you'll live close by the area you'll be hunting and can take advantage of some pre-season scouting trips. Physically scouting a location is by far the best measure of determining the quality of a hunting area, but by no means is it the tell-all predictor that many people think. Elk will act and react differently as hunting pressure mounts, activity levels in the area increase, and as weather and seasons dictate. I've taken some excellent scouting trips in areas that are literally brimming with elk, only to find the elk gone when I get to my spot on opening morning. It's important to understand your area and the amount of pressure it will get so that you can have appropriate plans and backup plans.

In the best of scenarios, the spots you find elk pre-season will remain undisturbed and you'll find elk there on opening morning. I have a theory that I call my elk "theory of halves", when I see 10 elk on a pre-season scouting trip, I'm likely to see 5 on opening day, then around 2 on the second day of the season, and one after that. I don't tend to stay in the same area past the second day of the season, I like to have an alternate plan.

How to scout

Many books offer different theories on scouting. Some believe that if you don't find fresh sign then you should rule that area out. Some believe that if you don't hear a bugle, you should move on down the trail and keep calling until you do. I'm somewhere in between. Understand that elk aren't going to act exactly the same way once hunting pressure is applied as they will before the season starts. You can pretty much bet that elk are going to move out of heavily pressured areas using any escape routes they feel safe in using. Elk are likely though to use the same game trails, benches, and saddles they use when moving from one area to another, so I prefer to find some better indications of elk activity prior to making an area my "spot."

Glassing

Glassing is my preferred method for making sure that elk are using areas that I'm interested in. This is where a good set of binoculars and some information from the local Game Warden will really pay off. I like to be out at the time I'll actually be hunting, early in the morning, to have a better chance at catching the movement of elk as they make their way from their nighttime feeding grounds to their bedding grounds. If possible, you should try to arrive the day before with enough light left to find large terrain features and the general path you'll take. Trying to find that ridge the game warden told you about while it's pitch black out isn't my idea of a good time. If you can find your way even almost to the spot, and mark on the GPS, you'll be a world ahead of the game the next morning when trying to navigate unknown terrain in the dark.

Once you're in your spot, spend quite a bit of time glassing all the areas you think may pay dividends, especially small meadows and openings where elk may still be feeding as the sun comes up. In the morning, you'll mostly be looking for shapes and movement; I like to glass a little more freely in the first hour of daylight, and then adopt what I've heard called a "grid" approach to analyzing the terrain. Getting used to glassing this way will be very helpful if your initial plans don't quite work as expected once hunting season starts. To glass in this manner, choose an area that should hold elk (remember all that we've learned about them, where they should be at a given time of day and season), and imagine a large grid over it. Begin focusing on one box of the grid at a time, picking apart each piece of landscape looking for "pieces" of elk, an antler, an ear, anything that might give away the location of an elk. Once you're satisfied that the grid you're inspecting is clear of elk, move on to the next and so on until you've covered the entire grid. Give your eyes a rest for a minute and then begin again.

Bugling

Depending on the time of year, bugling can help you to understand where the elk are in a given area, especially if the forest is dense. Bugling is best done over wide open areas like valleys and such where the sound will travel and the elk may respond with a return bugle. If you're in a heavily timbered area, bull elk may try to sneak in and look for you, or may just decide they'd rather not engage another bull and quietly move off without you ever knowing they were there. Be careful too about the kind of bugle you throw out there, there are locator bugles, and challenge bugles. I'll refer back to Paul Medel's series of CDs on bugling elk, if you really want to know the finer points of speaking their language and how to make a non-threatening locator bugle, you might want to buy Volume 1 of his CD set as a minimum.

Walking

Sorry, there's no way around it, you're going to have to put some miles on the boots while you're out scouting. The issue with many hunters and their scouting technique is that they cover areas by simply following forest or logging roads where elk are the least likely to leave sign. One of my hunting buddies and I once walked up such a trail to a beautiful spot on top of a mountain we had researched. On the way down, we decided to instead take a route that cut through the timber and back onto the trail about a half mile down the mountain. I was marking spots every 30 feet or so where there were wet, shiny elk droppings and trails converging all over the place. The spot was a backup spot since we didn't draw our preferred area, and low and behold the elk were easily called in on opening morning. We would have never realized the sheer numbers of elk in that area had we not gotten off the beaten path and walked where the elk do.

As you walk, try to remember how elk will traverse an area, they'll take the path of least resistance just like humans. The more ground you can cover by taking a route that is likely to cross many benches, hillsides, and saddles, the more game trails and heavily used areas you're likely to come across on your way. Once you find an area with many trails, follow the trails and look for droppings. I especially like to check around any areas where there may be dead trees lying across the trail as it seems that elk always take a pit stop when they come to one prior to crossing. Keep in mind, there are a few key things you're looking for when you're scouting:

1. Fresh droppings, the shiny kind that haven't cracked and are still wet from the elk, not from recent rains or morning condensation

2. Elk tracks: Remember to study them carefully, look at the edges of the track for signs of how old they are. Fresh tracks are crisp and the dirt and debris on the bottom are pressed into the ground. Older tracks have more rounded corners and may have debris from the wind settling within them. Tracks will also tell you which way the animal is going.

3. Converging game trails: Make sure you take advantage of every odds stacking technique that you can. Hunting one heavily used trail is good, but hunting a "hub" where multiple

game trails come together increases your odds significantly.

4. Elk sounds: As quiet as these animals can be, they can also be fairly noisy when walking through the forest cracking sticks as they go. One trick I have become attuned to is to listen for the chattering of squirrels. Squirrels will give a rapid chattering sound when they see something in the forest that they perceive as danger. I've been mighty tempted to put a 30.06 round through a squirrel at 5 yards on more than one occasion. I've since come to realize that the same squirrels that were giving away my location were also chattering as elk walked through the forest as well. Such sounds can be a good cue to slow down, move cautiously, and begin looking for nearby animals.

5. Elk: Walk quietly as you tread through the heavily timbered areas, looking around with every few steps for signs of elk. It's quite easy to see an elk before they see you in the early hours when they're preoccupied with feeding, so go slow, take your time, and don't forget that you're hoping to see elk! My confidence level always rises exponentially when I actually see elk using an area I'm interested in.

Have a Scouting Plan

You probably don't want to just walk into the woods and hope to stumble across some elk, always make sure you have a definite plan before you ever set foot out scouting an area. As frustrating as it can be to try to find the areas you've outlined on maps before the season, it's even more frustrating when the first hours of hunting season are ticking away while you try to figure out where to set up when you haven't decided on a spot. Just like you should have multiple plans when you set out to hunt, have multiple spots picked out prior to scouting and a well thought out plan of how you'll get from one to the other, and when you'll go to each.

My plans usually involve getting to a high ridgeline or some type of vantage point early in the morning, glassing for the first two hours of daylight. I then begin moving off to my B and C spots such as saddles or benches later in the day when I feel the elk will be bedded down. If my spots are a mile or so apart, I'll try to formulate a plan to get from point A to point B in either the fastest method possible if I'm limited on time, or through likely elk areas if I have the whole day and would like to multi-task as I walk and scout at the same time. Whatever is appropriate is fine; just try to formulate a realistic plan for spots to investigate, and routes between these areas.

Jumpstart Chapter 5

- There are four types of scouting: data, virtual, telephone, and physical. Try to use them all to your advantage
- Areas with higher resident success rates than non-resident success rates can be indicative of harvests mostly on private lands
- Try to choose an area where the effort required to hunt it is in line with your available time and physical condition
- Hunting pressure can be used to your advantage
- The reason most people don't find information they seek on the internet is they don't know how to look for it.
- Use the word "forum" in your searches to get more results from actual hunters posting in these
- Try to think of all the different names that an area might be referenced as when searching for information on it
- Use quotes around logically grouped words if you're not getting relevant results
- Google Earth allows you to scout areas very thoroughly using satellite images and topographical maps
- Elk are drawn to saddles as they're natural crossing points between higher elevation areas
- Finger ridges that face east tend to have more forage for elk than other areas due to greater moisture content, less sun exposure, and protection from harsh winds
- Draws offer secluded spots for elk to traverse hills while staying out of sight

- Hills and mountains offer elevated ground which can be cooler and offer relief from insects
- Elk love benches, they're easier to cross on, and offer comfortable areas that offer early detection of danger
- Valleys offer elk protected corridors to move through that keep them out of sight
- Game processing businesses and taxidermy shops may be good resources for getting valuable information about local areas
- Try calling fly fishing guides or local sporting goods stores when looking for information on an area
- Wildlife professionals respect hunters who have done their homework, the more prepared you are to speak to them, the better the quality of information you'll receive
- Try to avoid yes or no questions when interviewing Wildlife professionals, try to keep your questions open ended and specific as possible
- Physically scouting an area is the best way to assess the quality of a hunting area
- Remember that elk will react differently once hunting season arises and human pressure and activity increases
- Try to arrive the day before when scouting to ensure you can find large terrain features and trails when there is light
- Spend plenty of time glassing small meadows and openings in timber when the sun first comes up
- Bugling is best done over larger, wide open areas like valleys

where the sound will travel and elk may respond

- Look for easy escape routes, but try to cut across as many terrain features as possible when scouting
- Converging game trails will likely be good spots for stand hunting
- Listen carefully for chattering squirrels that give away the position of elk
- Have a scouting plan before you set out scouting, don't just walk aimlessly

Chapter 6: Out in the Field

Finally we've hit the point where the rubber meets the road. All the work that you've done prior to this will prepare you for the highest possible odds given your particular set of circumstances. You'll be well prepared physically and mentally with knowledge, appropriate gear, and a well formulated plan of attack.

All of this preparation will contribute to putting you in the best possible mental state for harvesting an elk. Hunting days can be long, and when you've been sitting in a treestand watching a trail hub for four or five hours without seeing an elk, it's easy to get discouraged, don't. Remember, all it takes is one elk walking through one of those trails to make your entire day memorable, so put in the time it takes beforehand to have the kind of confidence in the area you'll need. If you're faithful in doing so, you'll likely be out hunting when most of the other hunters are taking mid-day naps back at camp. So pack up your pack, grab your bow or rifle, we're off to the field where the fun really begins.

Common Sense

It may seem silly to have a section on common sense, but common sense is a big part of being successful as an elk hunter. I've watched many hunters over the years throw the most basic of hunting "knows" right out the window. Here are a few basic common sense items before we begin delving into some strategies and information related to being in the field:

- Don't increase activity levels needlessly in your hunting area – If you didn't have time to scout prior to the season, or you're hunting an area out of state that you couldn't get to prior to the hunt, it's acceptable to try to quietly explore the area looking for landmarks or trails that you've identified prior by virtual scouting. I've seen far too many hunters walking up trails, making excessive noise, and increasing the "signals" that will alert elk to the activity increase that will send them looking for private land. Try to keep the activity levels down whenever possible.

- Don't slam car doors, leave engines running, or speak loudly when arriving at your hunting destination by vehicle- This one is a pet peeve of mine. It's amazing how well the sound of the human voice carries and how you can hear a car door slam all the way up the side of a mountain. If you're arriving at your starting point by vehicle, remember to be as quiet as possible once you get there.

- Walk quietly into your area – Elk make noise when they move through an area and so do humans. I've had my adrenaline levels pumped up more than a few times after hearing what I thought were twigs snapping under an elk's hooves, only to find that it was a hunter moving slowly down a trail. Some noise is acceptable, but if your backpack is rattling, or you're tripping loudly through downed timber, an elk is more than likely going to get suspicious. Once you get close to your desired spot, slow down, place your feet solidly, and stop every once and a while like an elk would. You'd be amazed how close the animals can be without you ever knowing it.

- Don't camp right next to your hunting area or likely areas of other hunters – Some folks love to pack in for miles and set up camp, this can be an excellent way to cut miles off of your daily commute back and forth to camp. Wherever you decide to camp, try to be considerate to others and increase your odds by not setting up within a quarter mile of where you or others will likely be hunting. Even the quietest of people make way too much noise for elk not to notice.

- Don't set up too close to other hunters not in your party. If you get to your spot that you spent hours studying over maps to find and there's already a hunter there, be considerate and don't set up right by them, under them, or over them. I've seen more hunters do this, even to the point of setting up just below on a ridgeline they know another hunter is covering with his rifle. It's just plain stupidity and rudeness. If you need to execute plan B, do so and allow the other hunter a good enough amount of space to hunt, you'll appreciate it when someone returns the favor.

- Don't choose spots you can't physically get an elk out of – There are a few spots that I've heard about over the years that I know are just brimming with elk. The reason is that the paths to get down to them are amazingly steep and difficult to negotiate even without carrying fifty pounds of meat on your back. Know your limits and don't choose areas that are ridiculously difficult to get in and out of.

Morning Preparation

Being prepared to hunt in the wee hours of the morning will be a welcome departure from the usual clamoring around in the dark trying to figure out where you put your socks. If you've followed the methodologies outlined in the preparation chapter, then you should be well organized and ready to go quickly. Preparing your pack is a simple matter of re-filling your hydration bladder or water supply, grabbing a single sack of food for the day, and adding any additional clothing necessities you may need, such as extra layers or rain gear, in case the weather has changed since you loaded your pack.

Remember to add items to your pack in the reverse order of when you'll need them, such as loading extra clothing layers last so they're on top when you arrive at you spot and prepare for your body temperature to drop as you remain still. As you dress for your day's hunt, keep in mind that you'll most likely be walking a good distance and chances are you'll climb a hill or two on your way to your daily spot. No matter how cold it is, don't over-prepare by wearing three or four layers of clothing for the hike up the mountain. Once you get moving, your body temperature will rise rapidly and you'll find yourself drenched in sweat, not a good thing as morning temperatures drop and you find yourself shivering at your stand.

You should feel a little cold when you first start out, and keep those next layers of clothing handy at the top of your pack should you need them. You'll likely begin to get comfortably warm as you start walking, and can then easily throw on an additional layer or two once you reach your area. You'll be much more comfortable, warmer, and will have outer layers of clothing that aren't soaked with the smell of sweating human.

Slow and steady is preferable to keep your body temperature warm versus sprinting up the hill and becoming soaked with perspiration in the process.

Getting to Your Spot

You'll have to make sure you leave in time to get to your spot, and depending on hunting pressure, that may be a little earlier than most. If you have an excellent spot that you want to ensure nobody else gets to first, then you'll have to pay a little extra for it. Be prepared to rise a little earlier than usual and sit in the cold darkness for a little longer waiting for shooting light. If you're fairly certain that nobody else will be in the area you plan to hunt, there's little sense in arriving two hours before sunrise and shivering next to a tree until the sun comes up. Some hunters believe they need to let their area "cool down" after getting into position in case they made some noise getting set up. So long as you approach your area quietly, you should be able to get into position and become ready for a shot relatively close to legal shooting hours.

Setting Up Your Spot

If you've had the luxury of physically scouting and selecting your area before your hunt, you'll want to make sure to set up your area appropriately. Once you've chosen the spot you'll hunt from, perhaps due to the cover a particular tree or brush offers, or perhaps because there are many converging game trails on an escape route, you'll want to get it ready for the hunt. If you don't have the opportunity to visit your site ahead of time, you may wish to perform some of the following activities during mid-day when the elk are bedded down. The first thing I like to do is to clear the ground underneath where I'll be sitting. There may be dead branches, brush, pine cones, whatever the case may be, anything that might cause an inopportune crack or rustling under your feet if you have to change position for a shot. Next, sit in your spot for a moment and look all around you. Identify the most likely areas that elk will be coming through and analyze each one of them for issues that you can resolve.

This is very important, rarely does the perfect shot even present itself when hunting, but when a six point bull is standing 20 yards broadside to you with dead tree branches hanging right over his vitals, you'll wish you had taken the time to ensure you had clear shooting lanes. I often wondered how much a few small pine branches could deflect a bullet or arrow. I got my answer last year when my first shot of opening morning touched a very small dead pine branch and ran my broad head right into the ground. I found the arrow, but never found the broad head, it had snapped clean off. A little preparation beforehand can save you a lot of frustration and heartache later.

Game Plans

You should always have a morning, afternoon, and evening plan for your hunting. They may be all exactly the same, perhaps to sit in a tree stand overlooking a meadow for the entire day, so long as it's a conscious decision. You may wish to change tactics in the afternoon when elk are bedded down and not moving nearly as much or you may just want to change your calling routine during that time of day. I can almost guarantee that things won't happen the exact way that you picture them prior to the hunt, so be willing to change if the situation warrants it, just don't set out in the morning without a well thought out plan of how you'll address your day.

There are many different types of hunting strategies, the area, time of year, and how many hunters are in your party will likely dictate which you choose. My hunting buddy Jeff even has his own method called "Bump and run", where he says that he walks through the forest until he bumps into the animals accidentally and then watches them run away. Jeff, I'll give you credit; at least it's a strategy!

Stand hunting

Stand hunting is probably the most preferred of all the methods of hunting. Why? Well, I guess because it's the easiest and most relaxing. I'm not taking a dig into those who pick a spot and sit there all day, this is actually my preferred method of hunting in the mornings and evenings as I'd rather be very still and catch the elk's movement through an area. Stand hunting is typically more effective early in the morning and in the evening as these are the times that elk will most likely be moving to and from their bedding and feeding areas. Depending on the hunting pressure in an area, you may wish to stand hunt during the afternoon as well and let other hunters who are still hunting through bedding areas push the elk to you, it's your call. If you're stand hunting, prepare to sit for a long time and make sure you're as comfortable as possible. This is where I like to bring a small tri-fold stool to keep myself sitting comfortably and well off of the cold forest floor.

Still Hunting

If you're going to be still hunting, you'll have to have the patience for it, still hunting means moving so slowly, I'm talking taking a step as slowly as possible, then once your foot is down, scanning the terrain for any sign of an elk. After you're sure there's nothing in your vision that could be even part of an elk, you slowly take another step and scan again. I've heard jokes that the reason they call it still hunting is because you'll still be hunting when everyone else is back at camp. True perhaps, but this is a very effective hunting method and it will help ensure that you see the elk before the elk sees you. If this will be part of your strategy just remember to have patience. Elk will hold tight in an area and not move allowing hunters to walk right by them. It may take an amazing amount of patience, and re-examining areas you just looked at a few seconds before will become tedious. Here's the payoff, I've watched many times from higher vantage points as hunters made their way through a heavily forested area only to see animals move out well in front of them without their knowledge.

Still hunting is a great afternoon hunting method, if you can analyze a particular area, figure out where the animals are likely to be bedded (remember north and east facing slopes, upper third of hillsides, etc.), you can possibly find elk bedded down and execute a stalk or wait until they get up to feed. Keep in mind though that animals chased from their beds will likely leave the area completely. Sometimes it's better to try to harvest an animal at a different time of day or another day altogether versus running the risk of moving the animals out. If you have very limited time, your best bet will probably be to maximize every moment of hunting opportunity that you have and use this technique during the mid-day hours.

Spot and Stalk

To me, spot and stalk is the perfect alternative to still hunting, which I just don't have the patience for. For some reason, sitting in a spot and waiting takes less patience to me than moving slowly through the woods, go figure. Spot and stalk is exactly what the name entails, you get to a good vantage point where you can see much of the area, glass continuously until you find an animal, and then plan a well-executed stalk in order to get close enough for a shot. What I like about spot and stalk hunting is that when you do actually spot an animal, you'll know you're actually chasing something that is there, it makes the process of slowly stalking the animal much more appealing than still hunting where I'm stalking something that may or may not be in that area. You can also cover way more ground with your eyes than you can with your boots. The caveat is that the animals have to be moving or somewhere out in sight for you to spot them. This makes spot and stalk an excellent morning activity when animals aren't using the areas you identified on the map. By using this technique in the morning, you'll have plenty of time to plan an approach, wait for the morning air currents to die down, and execute your hunt.

Hunting Alone

Not everyone is fortunate enough to have a hunting partner, and sometimes life just happens, plans get changed, and you'll find yourself hunting alone in a particular area. Hunting alone presents some challenges to the hunter, and these challenges can be magnified depending on the season. In archery, it can be difficult to get animals to commit to coming in close enough to a call to get a shot. In rifle, it becomes difficult to effectively still hunt certain areas where animals may well have multiple escape paths that you can't cover alone. There are a few techniques you can use in your favor to help you in these situations. First, for the bowhunters, using a decoy is a very effective way to help give elk the confidence they'll need to come in close to your call. Elk are going to try to use every sense they have to confirm that it is in fact another elk making that noise and not a hunter. Having a decoy set up past where you are hunting, and on the other side of the trail from where you expect the elk to come from gives just another indicator to the elk that the sound is in fact real.

I really like to use the lost cow calls in these situations as these calls have pulled elk right to my hunting spot from a good ways off. One of the reasons I like to hunt the archery season more than rifle is the lack of hunting pressure. This of course is quite the opposite in the typical rifle season, and that's when the lone hunter can begin to take advantage of hunting pressure to move elk to him. Using other hunters as pressure requires a few changes in behavior for the hunter. You'll have to get up earlier than other hunters to ensure that you're in position on an escape route before they begin pushing the elk, and you also have to ensure that you're not the one doing the pushing.

Most hunters I've seen tend to carry on down the trail without a concern about factors such as wind direction. This can be used to your advantage if there are multiple ways into an area and you know most hunters will use the main trail. If you can identify the logical escape routes, you can plan for an approach that keeps the wind in your favor. This also allows you to not cross the path of areas you know elk will approach from and get into a perfect position to use the other hunters to push elk to you.

Jumpstart Elk Hunting

In the mid-day, depending on whether or not your area requires the use of hunter orange, you may wish to watch for hunters moving into areas to still hunt, and position yourself in safe areas that the animals could use as escape routes. When I say safe, I mean safe for you, not for the animal. If a single or group of hunters goes into a large stand of aspens with a funnel point at the end of it, covering the funnel point can yield excellent results. The hunter that pushes them to you is unlikely to know the animal was ever there. If the hunter is being very careful and still hunting effectively, he'll likely get the shot and you're none the worse for it. Use common sense if you use this method and make sure you're well out of the hunter's range and try to avoid being at the same elevation as where a hunter might be shooting. A miss on an animal could be a hit on you when the other hunter doesn't know you're covering logical escape routes so remember to be safe.

You'll likely have your best luck hunting alone by calling the animals in to you. Since you can't cover as much area, calling gives you the advantage of detecting movement or sound before the elk is too close allowing you to make any necessary adjustments for a shot. When hunting pressure heats up, elk are likely to limit their vocalizations to the nighttime hours so mews and breeding calls will draw suspicion. This is again where the lost cow call can be very effective. Elk get separated, it happens. It may be caused by predators, or just an elk not paying attention and feeding too far from the herd. Given the herding nature of these animals, lost cow calls tend to draw the elk out to lend a helping hand.

Hunting with a Partner

The best part about hunting with a partner is the fact that two people can cover twice as much area as a single person, unless of course they sit right next to each other. I see the latter happening all the time. Hunters from the same party tend to stick close together giving them almost the same level of effectiveness as a single hunter. If you are lucky enough to have a hunting partner or two, use this to your advantage. Think about the effective range of your weapon and make sure you're spread out by at least that much.

Also, if hunting using high powered rifles, make sure everyone is aware of where the other party members are. It is best if you can all plan your positions for an area, then keep to them when you set out. That way your hunting party will know where it is and is not safe to shoot. If you're hunting with bows, an effective range may be about 40 yards, so each hunter should have an 80 yard zone around them that they're covering. With high powered rifles with a 200 yard range, you may wish to do 100 yards apart as vision into the forest at this point begins to degrade your ability to spot animals passing between you.

Having a partner is very handy when it comes to still hunting. Still hunting with a partner allows you to effectively hunt a given area, and also use each other to push animals one way or the other, hopefully into the sights of your hunting partner. I like to call this zone hunting where each hunter covers the outer zones of a stand of timber where animals are likely to try to escape when

162

they sense human presence. Simply pick a point where you and your partner will meet up at the end of the area, then each hunter works slowly through the outer bounds of the area watching for animals either trying to escape from them or from their partner. Care must be taken in this type of hunting situation as well, especially if you cannot see the other member of your hunting party. Don't shoot when the animals are horizontal to your position and in between you and your hunting partner. Choosing a stand of timber like this is the best method for a pair of hunters to cover an individual section of their hunting area.

Hunting in a Party

Having multiple hunting party members gives hunters advantages that cannot be had with solo or even pairs of hunting partners. The classic maneuver for multiple hunters is to execute drives through stands of timber. This places the shooting hunters at the outer edges of the cover or likely escape routes in order to harvest animals as they attempt to sneak out of the area. Hunters that are performing the drive typically don't shoot unless they are 100% sure that there is no other hunter on the other side of the animal.

Covering escape routes and edges from different elevations can make this much safer, but the point is really to add human pressure to an area and harvest an elk on the way out of the timber. Have the hunting party decide who will be the shooters and who will be the drivers. Once the shooters are in position, the drivers spread out equally through the area covered and walk at a slow but steady pace. This is very different from still hunting in that the drivers have the intention of the elk knowing they are moving through an area. Keep in mind that techniques such as these work best in areas where the elk will be holding up, such as in bedding areas in mid-day.

Early mornings and evening hunts will do better with what I call "organized glassing." Party members spread out to cover multiple ridges and glass extensively. Good walkie-talkies are a necessity in this scenario as the idea is to relay the position of any sightings to the hunter closest to the elk. The guide can even talk the hunter right through the stalk, helping him adjust his route as the animal adjusts if the hunter can still be seen. This is actually a lot of fun for both the shooter and the guide as the guide shares in the excitement of watching the hunt unfold.

When to Hold Them, When to Fold Them

Impatience and elk hunting definitely do not go hand and hand. A lot of your decision to move on from one area to another will depend on your confidence level with the area, as well as the number of elk you witness moving through the area at a given time. Impatience or aggressiveness, they tend to be interchangeable in the elk hunting world so much of your decision will be based upon the length of your trip and the success that you witness in the area you're hunting. I've spent countless hours sitting in a stand waiting for an elk to walk by. It seems to take forever and I've found myself reasoning my brain out of an area, thinking about all the reasons why I might have gotten it wrong, when all of a sudden, poof! A few elk appear out of nowhere and my confidence is renewed.

I have a couple of good friends from Pennsylvania who come up almost every year to hunt. They're retired and can stay much longer than my hunting buddy and I. I always call John after I know they're home and even if they haven't filled, I most always get the scoop of how one of the two got a shot on day four or five after we've left. Persistence pays off, it only takes one elk to walk by your stand and your hunt can be a success. Remember that you'll likely diminish your odds significantly if you get impatient and begin wandering aimlessly through the woods.

There is a time though to face the grim fact that the elk may not be where you're hunting. Especially if you're hunting rifle season and you hear no nearby shots, or perhaps when you return to camp and speak with other hunters that didn't see elk in the area. At some point, if the elk aren't there, continuing to hunt that area will be about as productive as hunting elk in the Wal-Mart parking lot. Don't hunt where the animals aren't, you'll never be productive that way. Don't become emotionally involved with a spot because it looks like "perfect" elk country and just has to hold some elk.

Every year thousands of hunters are lured into perfect looking elk habitat, mostly because it looks like what they saw in a video or a magazine. If your elk hunting efforts aren't paying off, stop and go back to square one for a minute. Review all of the Jumpstart pages in this guide and begin analyzing your area. If after doing so you strongly feel you've made the right decision, then stick with it. If you see other opportunities and time permits, then by all means execute plan b, just make sure it's an actual plan b and you're not just wandering aimlessly through low odds areas.

The following list was designed as a sanity check for hunters to use when determining whether they are hunting in an area that should hold elk. If your current area isn't producing, and you feel that you've allowed sufficient time, go through the following sections and place a small check next to each factor that is true for your particular hunt and conditions. The more consistency the factors point to, the more likely the guidance will be correct. Altitude is the most varied here and hardest to pin down as you may be chasing elk anywhere from Idaho to California. Here in Colorado, highest range usually means 11,000 feet, mid-range is 8,000 to 9,000 feet, and lower is under 8,000 feet.

Altitude to Hunt
Factors:
- Season
    - Bow/Muzzleloader– Hunt highest range of altitude options
    - First Rifle -Hunt mid-range of altitude options
    - Later Rifle Seasons – Hunt lowest range of altitude options
- Temperature
    - Warm - Hunt highest range of altitude options
      Mild - Hunt mid-range of altitude options
    - Cold - Hunt lowest range of altitude options
- Snowfall
    - None – Hunt highest range of altitude options
    - 0-6" – Hunt mid-range of altitude options

    o   7-12" – Hunt lowest range of altitude options

Where to Hunt

Factors:

- Pressure
  - Heavily Hunted Public Land close to roads/camp – Outline escape routes, identify saddles, valleys, etc. that lead to safety (private land or rugged terrain)
  - Heavily Hunted Public Land away from roads/camps – Identify drainages, benches, thick forested areas near the upper 1/3 of 15-30 degree slopes
  - Lightly hunted private land – identify drainages, meadows near edges, benches
- Yearly rainfall to date
  - Low/Medium – Identify drainages with flowing water, small creeks, seeps, springs, ponds
  - High – drainages, small creeks
- Food
  - Early Seasons – Lower grasses/higher forbs and browse –
  - Late Seasons – Higher grasses/lower forbs and browse – follow food down snowlines if present
- Temperature
  - Hot – Hunt North and East facing slopes in upper 1/3
  - Mild - Hunt North and East facing slopes in upper 1/3
  - Cold – Hunt South facing slopes

How to Hunt

Factors:

- Season
  - Early Season
    - Vocal Elk – Hike high probability areas, use locator bugles, pinpoint response, get close and call
    - Non Vocal Elk – Hike high probability areas
      - Spot and Stalk through ridgelines
      - Still hunt through timber
      - Stand hunt along well used game trails
  - Late Season
    - Vocal Elk – Hike high probability areas, use locator bugles, pinpoint response and stalk
    - Non Vocal Elk – Hike High probability areas
      - Spot and Stalk through ridgelines
      - Still hunt through timber
      - Stand hunt along well used game trails
- Precipitation
  - Rain Coming – Hunt all day, glass from ridgelines to find elk feeding in anticipation of storm
  - Light Rain – No Change
  - Heavy Rain – Reconsider Hunting that day, typically low activity/movement – Still hunt thick timber with large over story
  - Post Heavy Rain – Spot and Stalk near food sources, utilize high areas with good glassing potential

- Pressure
  - High Pressure – Still hunt through dark timber in high probability areas
  - Low Pressure – Spot and stalk, utilize high areas with good glassing potential
- Lunar Phase
  - Full Moon – Elk feed all night, still hunt dark timber, afternoon hunt near water/food
  - Partial/New - Normal
- Time of Day
  - Early Morning /Evening– Spot and Stalk, utilize high areas with good glassing potential near probably feeding areas and between feeding/bedding areas
  - Mid-Morning/Afternoon – Still hunt, depending on time of year, call near bedding areas, set up near water sources, feeding sources

Jumpstart Chapter 6

- Don't increase activity levels needlessly in your hunting areas, elk will respond by moving
- Don't slam car doors, leave engines running, or speak loudly when arriving at your hunting area
- Walk very quietly through your area
- Don't set up too close to other hunters in an area
- Don't choose spots that you can't physically get an elk out of
- Make sure you leave camp in the morning with plenty of time to get to your spot, especially if you're counting on hunting pressure from hunters leaving later in the morning
- Prepare your spot as best you can beforehand if possible, clear ground where you'll sit, clear shooting lanes, remove possible obstructions.
- Always have morning, afternoon, and evening game plans for your day
- Bring a small tri-fold stool or the like if you're stand hunting to keep you comfortably off the ground
- Animals chased from their beds will likely leave an area completely, only hunt beds if you have very limited time and must make the most of very few days
- Glass extensively, you can cover way more ground with your eyes than with your boots
- Using a decoy if archery hunting alone can give the elk the confidence they need to come in closer
- Use other hunters and hunting pressure to your advantage,

identify entry points and logical escape paths and try to cut them off

- Lone hunters will likely have the best luck calling elk to them, lost cow calls can be very effective for this scenario
- Multiple hunters should split up and cover the effective range of their weapon and eyesight
- Multiple hunters can use drives to push elk out of areas and into the sights of their hunting party, just remember to be safe and make sure everyone understands where the other hunters are
- Use organized glassing techniques to cover much larger areas using handheld radios to convey locations to the closest hunter
- Have plenty of patience, but go to a plan b if no signs of elk are present (physical sign, gunshots, reports from other hunters)
- Don't hunt areas that just "look" like perfect elk areas, make sure you assess the area against elk behavior

Chapter 7: After Your Elk is Down

There's almost no feeling in the world I can describe compared to the pride, and to some extent relief, associated with kneeling down next to such a majestic animal that you just had the opportunity to harvest. It's the time in between the shot and the kneeling that really sucks. Unless you were fortunate enough to know exactly where you hit the elk and watched it fall in its tracks, you're going to go through a period of time where the "what if I can't find it", or "what if it was a bad shot" thoughts will creep into your mind.

There are a few things that you absolutely must do once you shoot an animal. The first thing to begin training yourself to do is to pick a feature that stands out very well right next to the area you know the elk was standing. This is so absolutely crucial whether you're bow hunting or rifle hunting, you must be able to identify where the animal was hit in order to decide what the next step you will take is. If you're a bow hunter, you'll likely think

172

you saw where the arrow hit and what happened to it. I can tell you this, I've been wrong just about every single time. Whether the hit was in a different spot than I thought, or at a different angle than I thought, or even this last year when I would have sworn that I watched the elk run off with the arrow sticking out the side, each time the "autopsy" revealed a different story. Rifle hunting is no different as you'll likely be much further away from your target. Whatever the case, make sure you immediately pick a tree, a rock, something that stands out right next to where you shot the animal and study it until you're 100% sure that you can identify it if you look away.

Most of the animals I've shot haven't gone too far, I've been pretty fortunate, but I've lost a few as well. Being able to perform a good analysis of the clues will help you understand if you need to give the animal some extra time or if you can begin your retrieval very quickly. Give the area at least 20-30 minutes to settle. This will be the hardest thing in the world as all the thoughts about losing your elk creep into your mind. Remember that the animal may not have gone nearly as far as you thought, so sit down, eat a sandwich or a snack, and give your projectile time to do its job.

Once you're ready to begin following the blood trail, walk over to the spot that you carefully marked when you made the shot. If it's several hundred yards away and you have a hunting partner, have he or she give you hand directions to ensure you get to the exact spot the hit took place, then begin looking for clues. If you're an archer, hopefully you'll find a bloody arrow lying on the other side of where the elk was. If you're a rifle hunter, begin looking for signs of blood and tissue matter on the ground. There are very important telltale signs of where and how you hit, so know the following scenarios:

- Blood with frothy tiny bubbles in it – This is a classic lung shot. Blood fills with small bubbles, sometimes only a few but the air will almost always leave some form of bubbles

- Blood with dark tissue in it – This is typically a heart or liver shot. Still an excellent hit, the fragmentation of the bullet can leave bits of tissue, either pink or dark red

- Blood with a strange stench to it, possibly signs of green slime – This is a gut shot. The animal will most likely lay down somewhere nearby, but death will take much longer than a vital hit

- No Blood – This one is tough, especially for an archer. Finding a bloody arrow will at least let you know you made a hit, but sometimes the arrow penetrates only partially and the shaft actually seals most of the wound. The same thing can happen with a bullet that makes a small entry hole and doesn't pass through.

What you find should determine what you do next. If it's one of the first two scenarios, you should be good to begin following the blood trail. I've followed blood trails for hundreds of yards that consisted of only a drop every few feet. Take your time. Take an arrow or a slim stick and place it in the last place you saw blood, then begin looking for the next drop in the direction you think the animal went. Once you find the next spot, move the stick or arrow to that spot. Continue doing this as you go, many times I've lost the trail and had to return to the point where I last found blood. Having that spot marked is very useful. If you can't find the next drop of blood, begin working in a spiral pattern, studying each spot on the forest floor working outward wider and wider until you've reached about 10 yards out. If you haven't found the next spot of blood, start over. There have been times when I've seen blood trails just mysteriously stop for no reason. At that point, once you've exhausted your circle pattern a few times, begin making 100 yard zig-zag patterns through the area. Make sure you're systematically covered the entire area, and if you still haven't found the animal, move 50-100 yards down from the last blood drop in the direction the animal was last heading and continue. Remember that animals tend to run downhill away from danger, so try to keep your search path heading in that direction.

If you happened to make a gut shot, the worst thing you can do is to push that animal. The first elk I ever took with my bow was a gut shot. I would have bet you every penny I own that it was a perfect double lung, but we followed the sparse blood trail further and further into the forest. We decided to give it a couple hours rest, then resumed at the last marker. We eventually found a small pool of blood another 200 yards into the forest by a small pine tree. Two hours hadn't been nearly enough, we ended up pushing that elk to the point that we never found it and the blood trail disappeared. We had found my arrow at the point I marked, later when I smelled it, it smelled awful. My buddies from Pennsylvania told me it was "gut juice." Had we left that elk alone 8 or

9 hours, and returned that evening, I would have likely found the elk in the spot where the blood was. Any signs of a gut shot should be given excessive time for the elk to die, these are amazingly resilient creatures and can go quite a long way if only wounded.

Gutless Method of Field Dressing

When I was little, I memorized an article from Outdoor Life magazine that had step by step instructions on how to field dress an animal. I knew exactly what to do and dreamt about performing the steps over and over. I took amazing care with my first few elk to ensure that every drop was removed from the body cavity. In the next section, we'll talk a bit about boning an animal out and why I believe strongly that it's a much better option, but for now, just know that the majority of the elk meat can be taken off without ever field dressing the animal. It gets the meat off the bone much quicker and aids in cooling the meat in the larger parts of the leg faster than if you were to gut the elk and then bone it out. There are some excellent videos on the internet where you can actually watch hunters perform this step by step, but the following is the general breakdown in case you have this book in the field and need to know what to do:

1. Roll the animal onto its back and position yourself at the rear of the animal, facing the front
2. Find where the rib cage ends by feeling upwards of the middle of the animal, move past the V of the rib cage up a few inches and make an incision that goes all the way to the rib cage

bone, about 1 inch long

3. I like a zip knife for the next step. A zip knife is an enclosed razor blade type knife with two finger holes in it. It allows the hunter to split the skin without worrying about cutting into the gut sack. Simply put the blade of the zip knife into the hole you cut and pull all the way down slowly cutting past the genitalia and almost to the anus. Make sure you do not cut into the membrane that houses the entrails. I've found this out the hard way, if it's hard to cut the skin, you haven't gone deep enough with the incision in step 2.

4. Lay your elk on one side. This is also the point where I like to put my plastic sheet under the elk prior to laying it down.

5. Return to the front part of the elk, and continue your cut from the rib cage straight up through the neck by the chin

6. Cut around the ankles of the animal where the joint bends on each rear leg, then the front legs. It's easiest (but not necessary) to break the joint and just remove the lower part of the ankle. If finding the joint is difficult, you may want to just saw through.

7. Slip your zip knife on the inside of each ankle where you just finished cutting around, and cut straight down to the incision you first made along the middle

8. Before I outline the next step, make sure you understand the regulations regarding naturally attached proof of sex. I've been told by Colorado Department of Wildlife personnel that leaving the scrotum or utters attached via membrane to a chunk of meat is fine. If this is the case in your area, make

sure to make this cut now so you don't forget.

9. Take your skinning knife and begin cutting away the skin from the meat, I like to do one side at a time starting from the rear leg until I get to the middle of the back. Cut with your knife angled like you were cutting almost into the skin, make long slashing strokes and it will come off easily.

10. Break the pelvic bone in the center of the elk by pressing the legs apart and begin cutting downward until you reach the hide. Once you've skinned the outside and cut any connective tissue, the entire leg will come off in a single quarter.

11. Pull back the front leg and begin working against the rib cage and into the meat until you find the joint. With a bit of work, you'll be able to cut the connective tissue between the joint, and the front leg will come off easily, just remember to cut close to the rib cage.

12. Follow the layer of meat over the ribs with your knife and remove this for the grinder. Again cut close to the rib cage to get everything off.

13. Find the backbone of the elk. Begin cutting, feeling your knife against the backbone at all times, all the way down the elk from the front quarter to the hind section. Make a second cut along the rib cage, once again feeling your knife against the bones of the ribs all the way along the same path you made the previous cut. This should yield a single large strip of meat known as the backstrap.

14. Work the meat up through the neck, cutting off chunks for the grinder.

15. Finally, the tenderloins can be accessed by reaching a small knife into the top rear section where you cut away the legs. You'll have to work your way past the membrane that holds the entrails in, and cut the meat where connected, about 12 inches back, to pull out each tenderloin

Using this method you'll waste very little if any meat. The ribs are a bit more difficult and can be stripped carefully without puncturing the entrails if you like. If you use the plastic sheeting I recommended in the chapter on gearing up, you can spread the sheet underneath the elk and have plenty of room left to set the leg quarters prior to boning them out. A little trick I like to use is to cut about 25% off of the sheet before I lay it out, that piece is used to cover any bags of meat that are placed in my pack thereby keeping the pack clean for the hike back to camp.

Boning out the meat

I'll never forget the first elk I ever killed and recovered. It was about 2 miles back through some pretty hilly terrain, however a large trail led up to almost the exact area I harvested her. We field dressed and quartered this rather large elk, taking back each quarter, the hide, and the head for CWD testing. We had a large game cart and my hunting buddy Bert and I took turns pulling 20 yards, then stopping to catch our breath. By the time we made it back to camp, that elk had almost killed us back. I wish someone had taken a picture of me back at camp because I know I looked about as beat up as any hunter has ever looked.

Once home, I set out to butchering the meat, removing it from the bones and throwing the scrap and bone into a large trash can next to my work area. When I was completely finished, I dragged a rather heavy trash can out to my side yard, realizing that I had carried all that weight through the mountains, only to remove it and throw it away. Needless to say, that was the last time I took an elk out without boning out the meat. If done carefully in the field, you'll reduce the weight of your load by about 30 percent and won't lose a drop of meat in the process. Make sure to check your local regulations, here in Colorado proof of sex must remain naturally attached to the animal. I still bone out most of my kill, however I'll keep the sex organ attached to a fully unskinned leg to remain legal.

Boning out hind legs is a fairly simple exercise. Most of the legs are made up of larger pieces of meat separated by a very thin layer of silverskin. If you examine the hind leg, you'll see the logical separations that will yield roasts and large chunks of meat to cut into steaks. It's hard to describe exactly how to do it, as a matter of fact, I have a hard time teaching people in the field without showing them. If you just pull apart the silverskin and cut at the bone where the meat is attached, you'll remove each large chunk of meat in a nice big piece that can be put into your meat bags (you did remember to bring pillow cases for meat bags didn't you?).

The front legs are almost as simple, however there's a single bone that runs horizontally along the front. If you follow that bone with your knife making a long cut, then cut downward along each side, you'll see where you have to follow the scapula along to remove one large chunk of meat. The rest of the cuts are very similar to the rear quarters in which you simply follow the silverskin. Put your meat into the meat bags immediately upon removal to keep them clean and you should be done with your task in no time.

The hide should also be in perfect shape for tanning if you so desire, and if you're removing antlers, simply saw across the top of the head making sure to take enough bone from the skull to keep the antlers together. I've packed out an entire small cow elk in one trip this way, maybe not the easiest trip back to camp, but I was thankful to only have to make one. Even if you're using a game cart to pull out the meat, you'll have a much easier time getting up and down the hills and over fallen timber if you're not carrying an extra 80-100lbs of waste. Once you do it this way, you'll likely never go back.

Keeping your Meat and getting it home

I have a rather large cooler, about 100 gallons in size that I use almost exclusively for keeping meat at camp and transporting the meat back home. It's very handy to get some bagged ice, however my meat was always wet once I got it home and moisture breeds bacteria so it's best avoided. One handy trick I now use is to get some large 1 gallon jugs, you can use empty washed out milk jugs or in my case, I've recycled some large containers of apple juice, filled them with water, and frozen them in my freezer. I have four of these and they're amazingly handy. They hardly melt at all due to their size and they keep the liquid inside the container as they melt keeping it away from your prized harvest. They're perfect substitutes for keeping your food chilled while on the trip and then serve double duty once the trip is over. Keep a couple near the bottom of the cooler, and place a couple on the top. Once you arrive back home, your meat should be cool and dry. Your meat will keep for several days in the case that you aren't leaving immediately or have other hunters in your party that haven't filled their tags yet.

Make sure you keep your coolers in a spot that will be in the shade as the sun moves across the horizon and you should have some excellent table fare once you arrive home.

Jumpstart Chapter 7

- Mark the spot with a landmark the second you hit the animal, make 100% sure you can find the exact spot the animal was standing when hit
- Assess the situation after the hit, make sure you give the animal plenty of time to expire based on what you find
- When tracking blood trails, place an arrow or stick where the last drop of blood was if you don't see the next one immediately
- Animals tend to run downhill to escape danger, if you lose the trail, try to pick it back up by looking for escape routes that lead downhill
- Any sign of a gut shot should be given excessive time for the animal to expire
- Gutless field dressing is easier, cleaner, and gets the meat off the bones quicker so heat can escape
- Boning out your meat will reduce the load you carry back to camp by 30% or more without losing any meat in the process
- Use 1 gallon plastic jugs filled with water and frozen to keep meat cool and dry when transporting
- Keep coolers filled with meat in an all-day shady spot to ensure lower temperatures

Conclusion

Each year that I set out to chase these creatures through the forest, I found that I've forgotten many of the pieces of information that I know will make a difference in my success. It's easy to fall back into old habits, to hunt the place you hunted years ago because it's familiar, even though you didn't fill your tag, to stick with an area you've chosen for days even though you haven't seen an elk, because there "just has to be elk here." At a minimum, review the jumpstart sections located at the end of each chapter as you begin planning your yearly elk hunt. These sections will hopefully jar some memories of the information you've learned and prompt you to take a more thoughtful approach to planning your hunt.

On average, a hunter will harvest a big game animal once every three years; you can most definitely beat those odds with just a little purposeful planning and knowledge about your area and the elk you love to chase. Elk hunting is hard work, it's not for the faint of heart, and you should be proud to call yourself an elk hunter. Put in the work, do everything you can to stay out in the field every second of hunting time that you have. I can promise you one thing; you'll never harvest an elk napping in a tent in the middle of the day. If you take nothing else from this book, please take with you an understanding of the importance of being prepared to stay the entire day in the field. Whether that means bringing enough food to keep you satisfied, multiple layers of clothing to keep you warm or cool enough in the field, or bringing a book to read to get you through the slow parts of the day, do whatever it takes.

One of my favorite aspects of hunting is the fellow hunters that I meet every year in the field and back at camp. From John and Barney, my faithful hunting friends from Pennsylvania, to my usual hunting partner Bert ("yotebait"), to Dave, Irene, and family who have adopted me in the field, fed me, and given me warm memories of my previous trips. If I were to never take another elk, I'd still cherish my time spent in the outdoors, hiking, hunting, and meeting fine folks such as you. Should you ever run across me in the field, stop and chat a while, as you can probably tell, we'll have lots to talk about!

Made in the USA
San Bernardino, CA
11 March 2018